Second Grade
FOUNDATIONS

GRADE 2

W9-BMN-292

American Education Publishing™
An imprint of Carson-Dellosa Publishing LLC
Greensboro, North Carolina

American Education Publishing™
An imprint of Carson-Dellosa Publishing LLC
P.O. Box 35665
Greensboro, NC 27425 USA

ISBN 978-1-62399-078-7

02-147137784

Table Of Contents

Table Of Contents

Table Of Contents

Table Of Contents

In second grade, your child will advance beyond the basic skills of kindergarten and first grade, as those skills are now being used with ease. Your second grader's attention span is expanding, which allows him or her to understand and apply more difficult concepts. Second graders are better at processing information, and they are learning to build on the things they know to understand more about them.

Second Grade Foundations offers activities for a full year of practice. The practice pages are simple and engaging, providing hours of learning fun. Many activities also connect with science or social studies for a wide range of learning. With *Second Grade Foundations*, your child is getting a well-rounded supplement to his or her education.

Language Arts

By the second grade, your child has probably mastered reading and writing at a basic level. Now, he or she will tackle more and more texts with an emphasis on becoming a fluent reader. With *Second Grade Foundations*, your child will gain a full year of practice with these important skills and will therefore develop greater confidence and understanding.

In second grade, your child will learn:

- to decode words with common prefixes and suffixes. **pages 22–23**
- to use pronouns. **page 30**
- to use an apostrophe to form contractions and frequently occurring possessives. **page 49**
- to identify the main purpose of a text, including what the author wants to answer, explain, or describe. **pages 59–64, 69, 85**
- to compare and contrast the most important points presented by two texts on the same topic. **pages 61–62, 74–75**
- to ask and answer such questions as who, what, where, when, why, and how to demonstrate understanding of key details in a text. **page 92**

Use the following hands-on activities to practice language arts skills with your child. These activities encourage creativity and logical thinking. Keep in mind that the process, not the finished product, is what is important!

- Encourage your child to create more varied and interesting sentences by substituting words he or she uses repeatedly with synonyms. As your child reads his or her writing to you, point out places where a synonym might be used, such as the use of the words *tiny* or *small* instead of *little*.

• Challenge your child to find words in newspapers, magazines, or catalogs that fit a certain phonetic pattern, such as short vowels with the **an** sound or words with the **long e** sound. He or she can cut and glue words with like patterns on separate pieces of paper, and join them to make a phonics book.

Math

Math concepts become more complex in the second grade. Second graders will learn to add and subtract two-digit numbers and to understand the meaning of multiplication and division. With *Second Grade Foundations*, your child will practice math skills that are fundamental to learning these concepts. These skills will provide building blocks for the years of schooling to come.

In second grade, your child will learn:

• to understand that the three digits of a three-digit number represent amounts of hundreds, tens, and ones. **pages 98–101**
• skip-counting by 2s, 5s, and 10s. **page 105**
• to compare two three-digit numbers based on meanings of the hundreds, tens, and ones digits. **pages 106–107**
• to add and subtract within 1,000. **pages 108–112, 114–126**
• to use addition and subtraction within 100 to solve one- and two-step word problems. **pages 110, 112, 116, 123**
• to solve word problems involving dollar bills, quarters, dimes, nickels, and pennies, using $ and ¢ symbols appropriately. **pages 127–132**
• to tell and write time from analog and digital clocks to the nearest five minutes, using A.M. and P.M. **pages 160–163**

Your child will become more interested in math if he or she can see how it applies to life outside of school. Here are fun ways to practice age-appropriate math with your child throughout each day:

• Make up skip-counting rhymes. For example: "2–4–6–8, what's the state that's really great?" or "1–3–5–7, can you count to one hundred eleven?"
• If you give your child an allowance, encourage him or her to save for items he or she wants. From time to time, help your child count the money he or she has saved. Ask questions such as, "How much have you saved so far? How much money do you still need?"

Language Arts

1. Reading is my favorite hobby.

DICTIONARY

three

hen   beach

yes   mess   peach

pet   tree

Whistle While You Work

Directions: Look at the first picture in each row. Circle the pictures that have the same beginning sound.

1. wh
   whistle

2. sh
   shoe

3. ch
   chin

4. th
   thumb

Try This!

On another sheet of paper, write three words that end with the *sh*, *ch*, and *th* sounds.

10

Make a Word

Directions: Write **str**, **shr**, or **thr** to complete each word. Then, write the word on the line.

1.  _____ ong _____

2.  _____ ub _____

3.  _____ one _____

4.  _____ unk _____

5. 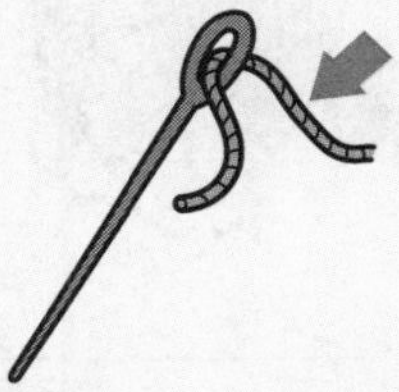 _____ ead _____

6.  _____ ap _____

Try This!

If you were a king or a queen on a throne, what rules would you make for your school? List them on another sheet of paper.

11

Fun with Final Sounds

Directions: Write the word that rhymes with each word below.

 1.

clock

_____

2.

hatch

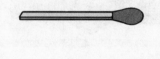

_____

3.

luck

_____

4.

batch

_____

5.

snack

_____

Try This!

Besides a clock, name other tools used to tell time.
List them on another sheet of paper.

Inching Along

Directions: Color the space yellow if the word has the **long a** sound. Color the space purple if it has the **short a** sound.

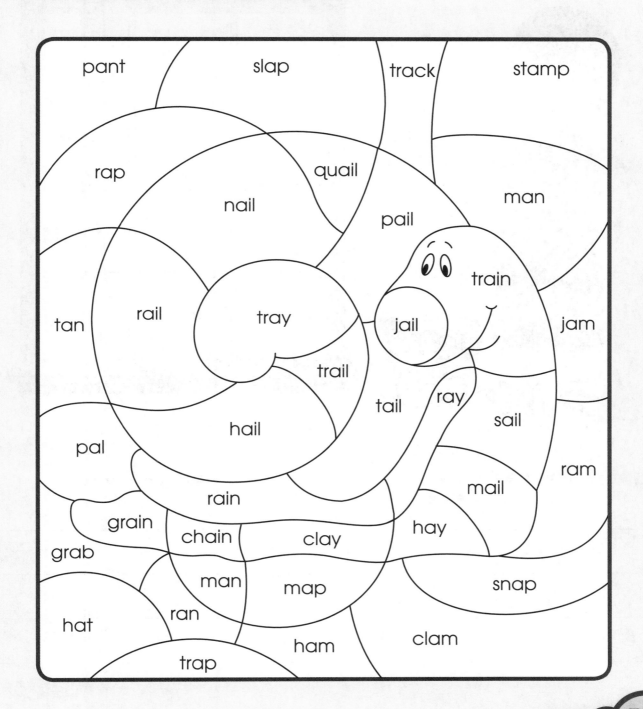

On another sheet of paper, write five more words that have the long a sound and five more words that have the short a sound.

Try This!

An Easy Mess to Clean

Directions: Write the words under the correct heading.

	three	
	hen	beach
yes	mess	peach
pet	tree	

Short e Words   **Long e Words**

_____   _____

_____   _____

_____   _____

_____   _____

Try This!

On another sheet of paper, write a story about a big mess that needs to be cleaned up.
Use at least two short e words and two long e words in your story.

Shining Stars

Directions: Say each word. Color the stars with the **short i** sound green. Color the stars with the **long i** sound yellow.

1.

trick

2.

ride

3.

bike

4.

spill

5.

lion

6.

kite

7.

lip

8.

kick

9.

lime

Try This!

Write two numbers that have the long i sound and one number that has the short i sound on another sheet of paper.

15

A Note for Fox

Directions: Write the word from the word bank that names each picture.
Write one letter in each box.

rose	rod	stove
frog	rope	fox

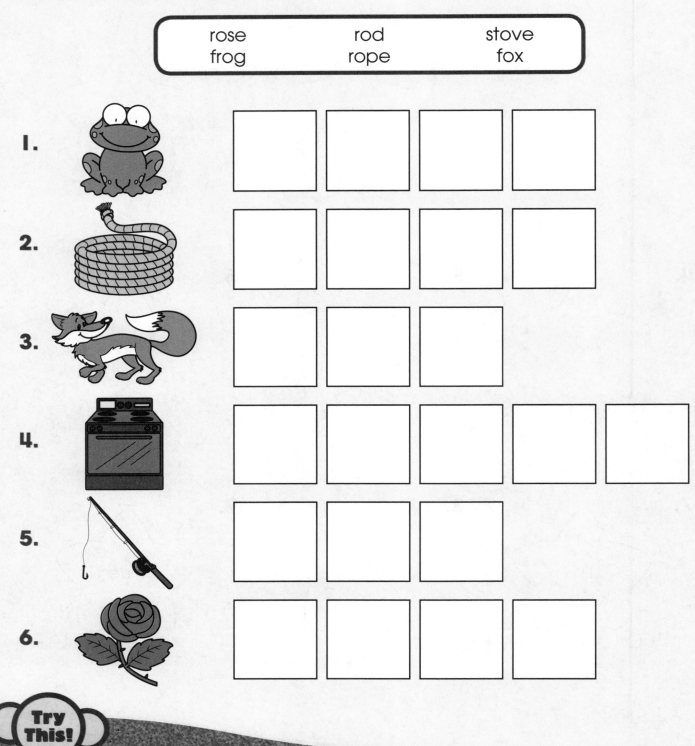

What a Cute Duck

Directions: Cross out the word in each row that contains the **short u** sound.

1. cute   duck   tune

2. suit   mute   tub

3. cube   truck   juice

4. fuse   amuse   cluck

5. dune   use   doughnut

6. club   tube   huge

7. cut   flute   rule

8. fruit   luck   mule

Try This!

On another sheet of paper, write one sentence using as many of the words above as you can.

Touchdown!

Directions: Write each word under the correct heading.

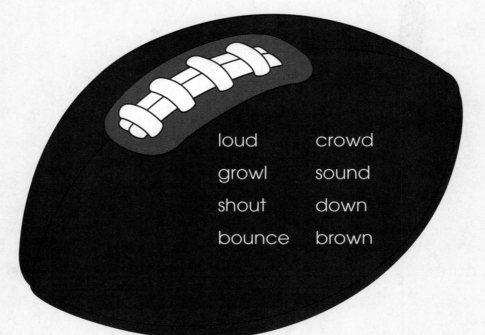

loud   crowd

growl   sound

shout   down

bounce   brown

ou Words   **ow Words**

_____   _____

_____   _____

_____   _____

_____   _____

Try This!

On another sheet of paper, make a Venn diagram showing how soccer and football are alike and different.

The Book Nook

Directions: Write the words on the correct page in the book.

look	school	wood	room
book	zoo	hook	goose

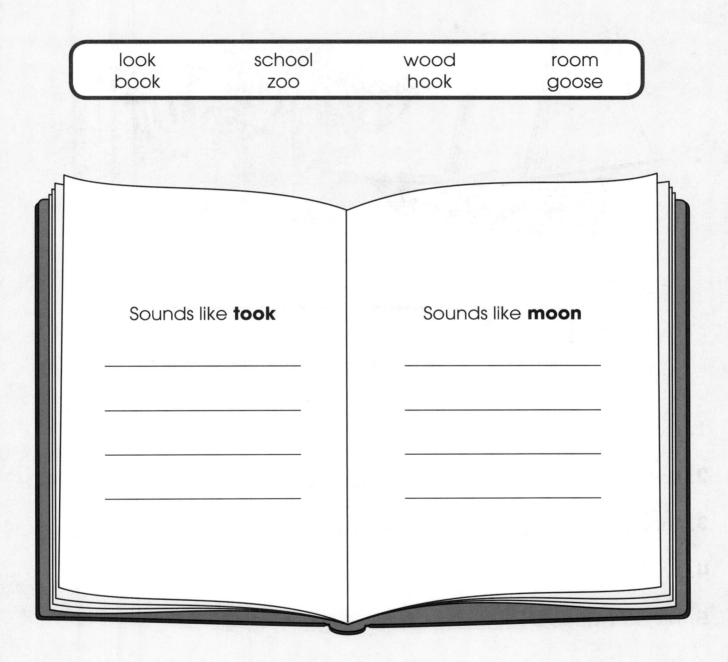

Sounds like **took**

_____

_____

_____

_____

Sounds like **moon**

_____

_____

_____

_____

Try This!

Design a book cover for your favorite book.
Be sure to include the author's name and a drawing that shows what the book is about.

Ship Ahoy!

Directions: Write a word to complete each sentence.

coin	soil	choice
boy	joy	toy

1. I found a shiny _____ on the island.

2. It was buried in the _____.

3. That _____ is my brother.

4. We had a _____ of fish or coconuts.

5. My dad made a _____ out of string.

6. We jumped with _____ when we saw the ship.

Try This!

An island is a piece of land that is surrounded by water on all sides. Look at a map. List some islands that you find on another sheet of paper.

It's a Snap!

Directions: Snap out the syllables as you read each word. Write the number of syllables in each word.

1. apple _____

2. donkey _____

3. pudding _____

4. cat _____

5. oven _____

6. bread _____

7. dog _____

8. pizza _____

9. milk _____

10. orange _____

11. cheese _____

12. puppy _____

Try This!

On another sheet of paper, make a list of 10 words with one syllable and a list of 10 words with two syllables.

Prefix Party

Directions: Read the prefixes and their meanings. Then, write the correct prefix in each sentence.

Prefix	Meaning	Example
bi-	two	bicycle
un-	not	unhappy
re-	again	rebuild
pre-	before	preschool

1. Our meeting is every two weeks. It is _____ weekly.

2. Before reading a book, I like to _____ view the cover.

3. Since he had five questions wrong, he had to _____ take the test.

4. Candy is an _____ healthy snack.

Try This!

Why do you think *preschool* is called *preschool*? Explain on another sheet of paper.

Half Full?

Directions: Read the clue. Then, use suffixes **-ful** or **-less** to make a new word.

Clue	New Word
1. full of joy	_____
2. without color	_____
3. full of hope	_____
4. full of grace	_____
5. without care	_____
6. without sleep	_____
7. full of delight	_____
8. full of power	_____

Try This!

On another sheet of paper, write a paragraph using at least three of the new words above.

Someone Who . . .

Directions: Use the words in the word bank to answer each question. Underline **or** or **er** in the answer.

author	baker	catcher
doctor	illustrator	photographer

1. A person who bakes is called a _____.

2. When you are sick, you should visit a _____.

3. An _____ writes the words in a book.

4. A _____ is the person who catches the ball in his glove.

5. A _____ uses a camera when she works.

6. If you like to draw pictures, maybe you will become an _____.

Try This!

Can you identify more jobs that end with *-er* or *-or*?
Make a list on another sheet of paper.

Nifty Nouns

Directions: Write each noun in the correct column.

NOUNS

car	statue	desk	school
teacher	mother	ball	baby
Washington	cave	doctor	playground

PERSON	PLACE	THING

Try This!

Make a chart like the one above on another sheet of paper. Write five more nouns in each column.

Perfectly Proper Nouns

Directions: Write each proper noun on the line. If the word is not a proper noun, cross it out and write a proper noun for the word.

1. movie _____

2. Tisha _____

3. state _____

4. school _____

5. principal _____

6. country _____

7. Atlantic Ocean _____

8. friend _____

Try This!

List at least five more states on another sheet of paper. If you get stuck, look for a resource to help you.

More Than One

Directions: Write **s** to make each noun plural.

1. chicken _____

2. horse _____

3. fence _____

4. shovel _____

5. duck _____

6. egg _____

7. cow _____

8. haystack _____

On another sheet of paper, finish the story:
When I walked into the barn, I couldn't believe my eyes!

Pesky Plurals

Directions: Write **es** to make each noun plural. Then, use two of the words to write a sentence.

1. fox _____

2. bush _____

3. bus _____

4. lunch _____

5. sandwich _____

6. box _____

_____

_____

_____

_____

_____

_____

Try This!

Write another sentence using two different words from above.

More Than One Fun

Directions: Write the correct plural of each word in the puzzle.

Across

1. foot

5. child

7. person

8. half

9. wolf

10. loaf

Down

2. tooth

3. mouse

4. shelf

6. wife

Try This!

Write five sentences using words from the puzzle.

Pronoun Pride

Directions: Replace the underlined words in each sentence with a pronoun. Write the pronoun on the line.

1. <u>That girl</u> can dance. _____

2. <u>My brother</u> likes to bake cakes. _____

3. <u>The bicycle</u> is really cool. _____

4. <u>Jayla and I</u> are gymnasts. _____

5. <u>Quan and Reese</u> won their soccer game. _____

6. <u>The ball</u> sailed over the fence. _____

Make a list of eight pronouns.
Use each pronoun in a sentence.

Camping Action

Directions: Underline the action verb in each sentence.

1. Miguel and Marisa gathered some wood.

2. Papa built a fire with the wood.

3. Soon, the fire blazed.

4. Papa peeled the bark of two green branches.

5. He handed one to each child.

6. They roasted marshmallows.

Try This!

Write step-by-step directions for making s'mores with your family over a campfire.
Be sure to include action verbs.

Fishing for Verbs

Directions: Read the sentence in each fish and circle the verbs. If the verb shows action, circle the fish in blue. If the sentence does not show action, it has a linking verb. Circle the fish in green.

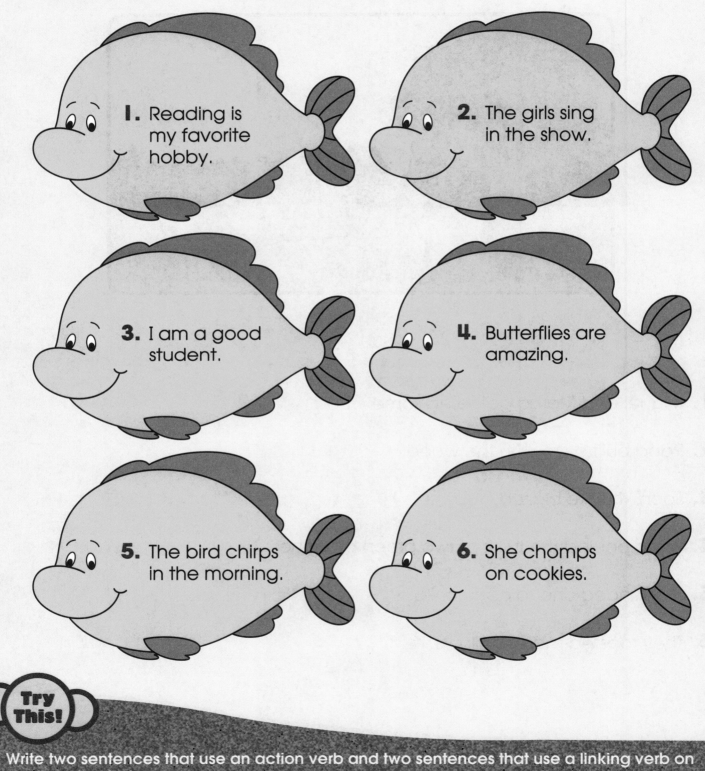

1. Reading is my favorite hobby.

2. The girls sing in the show.

3. I am a good student.

4. Butterflies are amazing.

5. The bird chirps in the morning.

6. She chomps on cookies.

Try This!

Write two sentences that use an action verb and two sentences that use a linking verb on another sheet of paper.

Animal Actions

Directions: Choose the correct verb. Write it on the line.

1. The monkeys _____ from branch to branch. (swings, swing)

2. The puppy _____ on the kids. (jump, jumps)

3. The kittens _____ with the string. (play, plays)

4. The penguins _____ on the ice. (slide, slides)

5. An owl _____ at night. (hoot, hoots)

6. The rabbit _____ into the hole. (hop, hops)

7. The horse _____ in the pasture. (gallop, gallops)

8. The squirrels _____ up the tree. (scamper, scampers)

Try This!

Write three more sentences about animals. Include an action verb in each sentence.

Actions in the Past

Directions: Write the correct past tense verb on the line.

1. I _____ the floor yesterday. (sweeped, swept)

2. He _____ a picture of a duck. (drew, drawed)

3. Dad _____ dinner for us. (maked, made)

4. I _____ to the store. (goed, went)

5. The children _____ in the next room. (slept, sleeped)

6. The bears _____ into the woods. (runned, ran)

7. He _____ across the lake. (swimmed, swam)

8. Grandma _____ to visit. (came, comed)

Try This!

Write a paragraph about what you did yesterday.
Use at least two verbs that do not use -ed to tell about the past.

Seeing Double

Directions: Double the consonant and write either **ed** or **ing** at the end of each word.

> Sit = Sitting   Step = Stepped

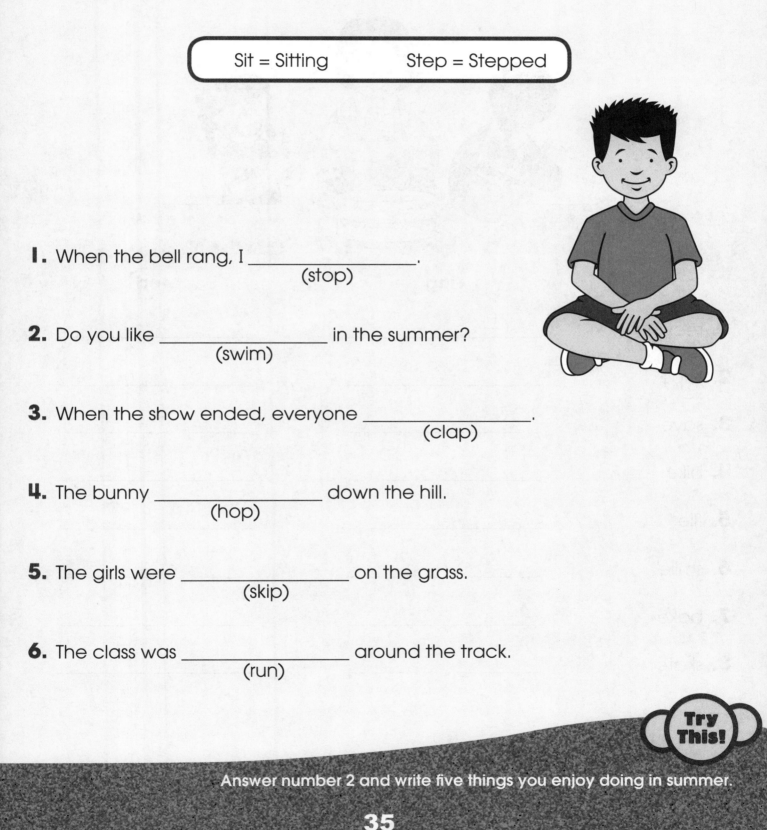

1. When the bell rang, I _____.
(stop)

2. Do you like _____ in the summer?
(swim)

3. When the show ended, everyone _____.
(clap)

4. The bunny _____ down the hill.
(hop)

5. The girls were _____ on the grass.
(skip)

6. The class was _____ around the track.
(run)

Try This!

Answer number 2 and write five things you enjoy doing in summer.

Go Green: Recycling!

Directions: Write the suffixes at the end of each word. Write the new words on the lines. Circle the letter that you "dropped."

	+ing	+ed
1. recycle	_____	_____
2. tape	_____	_____
3. save	_____	_____
4. bike	_____	_____
5. file	_____	_____
6. smile	_____	_____
7. bake	_____	_____
8. skate	_____	_____

Try This!

On another sheet of paper, list reasons to recycle.

Today's News

Directions: Write **is**, **am**, or **are** in the sentences below. These words tell us that something is happening now.

1. We _____ going on vacation.

2. My grandparents _____ moving next door.

3. I _____ tired today.

4. That child _____ a good dancer.

5. The cat _____ sleeping in the sun.

6. Do you think I _____ late for dinner?

Try This!

Write three sentences using *is*, *am*, and *are* on another sheet of paper.

Music to My Ears

Directions: Underline the correct linking verb in each sentence.

1. Some children (was, were) late for music class.

2. Jose (was, were) the first to arrive.

3. Kami and Javon (was, were) the last to come.

4. Finally, the children (was, were) in their seats.

5. The teacher (was, were) at the front of the class.

6. The boys (was, were) on their best behavior.

7. Beth, Byron, and Carlos (was, were) happy.

8. The teacher (was, were) pleased with the children.

Try This!

Write a sentence about music using the word *was.*
Then, write another sentence about music using the word *were.*

Sensible Food

Directions: Write one word in each space to describe the food. The first one is done for you.

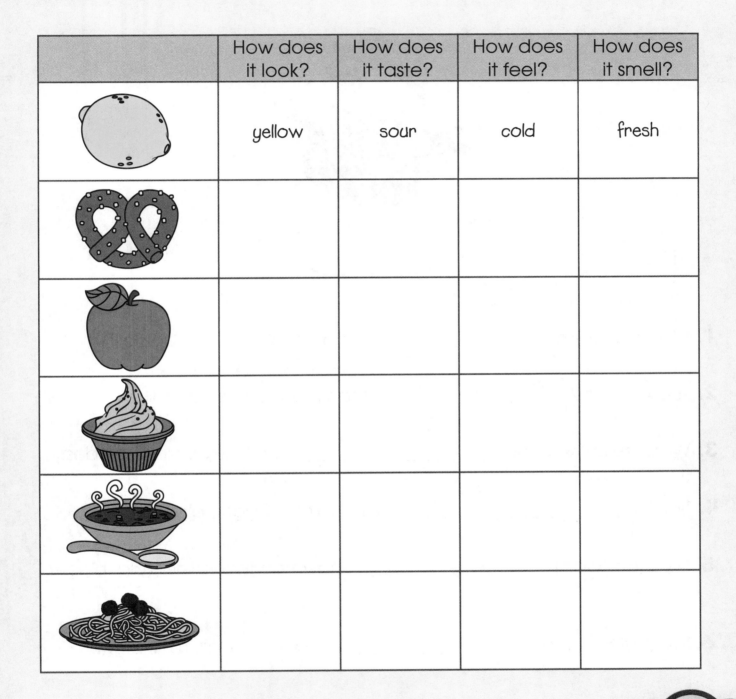

	How does it look?	How does it taste?	How does it feel?	How does it smell?
	yellow	sour	cold	fresh

Try This!

On another sheet of paper, write four adjectives to describe your favorite food.

Snuggle Up!

Directions: Write the correct word to complete each sentence.

1. Monday was a _____ day. (cold, colder, coldest)

2. Tuesday was _____ than Monday. (cold, colder, coldest)

3. Wednesday was the _____ day. (cold, colder, coldest)

4. I built a _____ snowman. (big, bigger, biggest)

5. My sister built a _____ snowman than mine. (big, bigger, biggest)

6. My dad built the _____ snowman of all. (big, bigger, biggest)

Try This!

Make a plan for a snow day. What will you do? What will you eat?
Write your plan on another sheet of paper.

An Apple a Day

Directions: Write the words in the correct space.

| apple | orange | pear | kiwifruit |
| banana | apricot | lemon | avocado |

A   **An**

_____   _____

_____   _____

_____   _____

_____   _____

Try This!

On another sheet of paper, write a paragraph describing your favorite fruit without telling the name of the fruit. See if your friend can guess what your favorite fruit is.

Camp Rules

Directions: Rewrite each sentence correctly.

I. breakfast is at 7:30 each morning

_____

2. you must clean your cabin

_____

3. every camper needs a buddy

_____

4. three campers can ride in a canoe

_____

5. all lights will be out at 9:00

_____

Try This!

Choose one rule from above.
On another sheet of paper, write why the rule is a good or bad idea.

Scrambled Sentences

Directions: Unscramble the words to make a sentence. Write the sentence on the line.

1. like I hike to

_____

2. birthday is my Today

_____

3. solve to mysteries Sarah likes

_____

4. my bee stung finger The

_____

5. My is nurse mother a

_____

Try This!

Write five sentences on sentence strips. Cut apart the words and see how many sentences you can make with the words. Write the sentences on another sheet of paper.

Small Talk

Directions: Rewrite the questions correctly.

1. how old are you

_____

2. are you in second grade

_____

3. who is your teacher

_____

4. what is your favorite book

_____

5. where do you live

_____

Make a comic strip about you and a friend talking on the phone.

44

That's Exciting!

Directions: Read each sentence. If the sentence shows excitement, write an exclamation mark. If not, write a period.

1. I am so excited

2. Our team won the game

3. My brother is on the team, too

4. My friend watched the game

5. We received a huge trophy

6. Then, we went for pizza

7. I ate a piece of pizza

8. Today was the best day ever

Try This!

On another sheet of paper, write three sentences telling about something exciting.

A Picnic Lunch

Directions: Insert commas where needed. You should have 12 in all.

1. Davis Destini and Dylan went on a picnic.

2. They brought a basket a blanket and a radio.

3. They ate sandwiches pickles and fruit.

4. They saw Emory Juan and Brian hiking.

5. They flew kites walked and gathered flowers together.

6. They want to plan another picnic for Sunday Monday or Wednesday.

Try This!

Write a story about a special time you shared with a friend.
Illustrate your story.

Dear Friend

Directions: Read the letter. Then, follow the directions.

January 22, 2011

Dear Blane,

On Saturday, I am going to my grandmother's house. We are going sledding. Then, we will bake cookies and make hot chocolate. After dinner, we're going to snuggle on the couch and watch a movie. What are you going to do on Saturday? Write me back.

Your friend,

Colby

---

1. Underline the date.

2. Circle the closing of the letter.

3. Draw a box around the body of the letter.

4. Draw a squiggly line under the signature.

5. Draw a star by the greeting of the letter.

Write a letter to a relative. Ask an adult to help you address an envelope and mail the letter.

Quotation Station

Directions: Underline the exact words spoken in each sentence. Then, put quotation marks around the quotation.

1. The train is here! exclaimed Justin.

2. Can we get on the train? asked Cara.

3. Not yet, warned Mrs. Rossi.

4. All aboard! shouted the conductor.

5. Now we can get on the train, said Mrs. Rossi.

6. Tickets, please, said the conductor.

7. Here are our tickets, said Mrs. Rossi.

8. I love riding the train, said Justin.

9. Me too! agreed Cara.

10. Can we ride it again tomorrow? asked Justin.

Try This!

Write a conversation you had with a friend.
Be sure to include quotation marks around the words that were said.

At the Park

Directions: Read the sentences. Make a contraction out of the words under each line. Circle the letters that the apostrophe takes the place of.

1. _____ going to the park to play.
   <u>We are</u>

2. Porchia and her brother _____ go.
   <u>cannot</u>

3. _____ going to swing on the bars.
   <u>I am</u>

4. _____ run too close to the swings.
   <u>Do not</u>

5. Becky _____ having fun.
   <u>is not</u>

6. _____ going to teach us a new game.
   <u>She is</u>

7. _____ like the new game.
   <u>You will</u>

8. _____ fun to play at the park.
   <u>It is</u>

Try This!

On another sheet of paper, write about a fun day at the park.
Use three contractions in your writing.

School's Out

Directions: Read the letter below. Circle each word that should be capitalized.

june 5, 2011

dear aunt amy,

my last day of school was friday. mom and i are going to orlando, florida. in july, i am going to visit uncle roberto in new york. we are going to see the statue of liberty on independence day. are you taking a vacation this summer?

yours truly,

anton

 Try This!

On another sheet of paper, write a letter to someone telling him or her what you would like to do during your summer break. Capitalize the words if needed.

Surprising Synonyms

Directions: Read the sentence that tells about the picture. Circle the word that means the same as the bold word.

1.

The child is **unhappy**.

sad   hungry

2.

The flowers are **lovely**.

pretty   green

3.

The baby was very **tired**.

sleepy   loud

4.

The **funny** clown made us laugh.

silly   glad

5.

The ladybug is so **tiny**.

small   red

6.

We saw a **scary** tiger.

frightening   ugly

Try This!

Use a thesaurus to find synonyms for the word *happy*.
Write the words you find on another sheet of paper.

Opposites Attract

Directions: Rewrite each sentence using an antonym in place of the underlined word.

1. My teacher <u>found</u> a box of magnets.

_____

2. Those two objects moved <u>together</u>.

_____

3. Cory <u>filled</u> the bucket.

_____

4. We used <u>hot</u> water for the experiment.

_____

5. That boat <u>floats</u>.

_____

Make a list of five more pairs of antonyms.
Use each antonym in a sentence.

You're Invited!

Directions: Complete each sentence using **your** or **you're**.

1. _____ invited to my sleepover.

2. Please bring _____ sleeping bag.

3. _____ welcome to bring a game.

4. You can bring _____ favorite CDs, too.

5. _____ going to love my new room.

6. I took some ideas from _____ room.

7. Have _____ mom drive you to my house.

8. I hope _____ able to come.

Try This!

Write five sentences on another sheet of paper.
Use both *your* and *you're* in each sentence.

A Terrific Trio

Directions: Complete each sentence using **their**, **they're**, or **there**.

1. Do you see those boys over _____?

2. _____ triplets.

3. _____ names are Carson, Carter, and Cameron.

4. _____ on the same baseball team.

5. _____ all good players.

6. _____ team won the game.

7. _____ dad is the coach.

8. He is standing over _____.

Try This!

On another sheet of paper, write a paragraph about what you think it would be like to be part of a set of triplets.

The *Two, To, Too* Crew

Directions: Complete each sentence using **two**, **to**, or **too**.

1. The team is going _____ row the boat.

2. The race is in _____ days.

3. They hope _____ win the race.

4. Those _____ children are on the team.

5. Don't let _____ many in the boat!

6. It is _____ windy to row the boat.

Try This!

Use *to*, *two*, and *too* in one sentence.
Write it on another sheet of paper.

Compound Connection

Directions: Read the sentences. Fill in each blank with a compound word from the box.

raincoat	bedroom	sandbox
hallway	notebook	

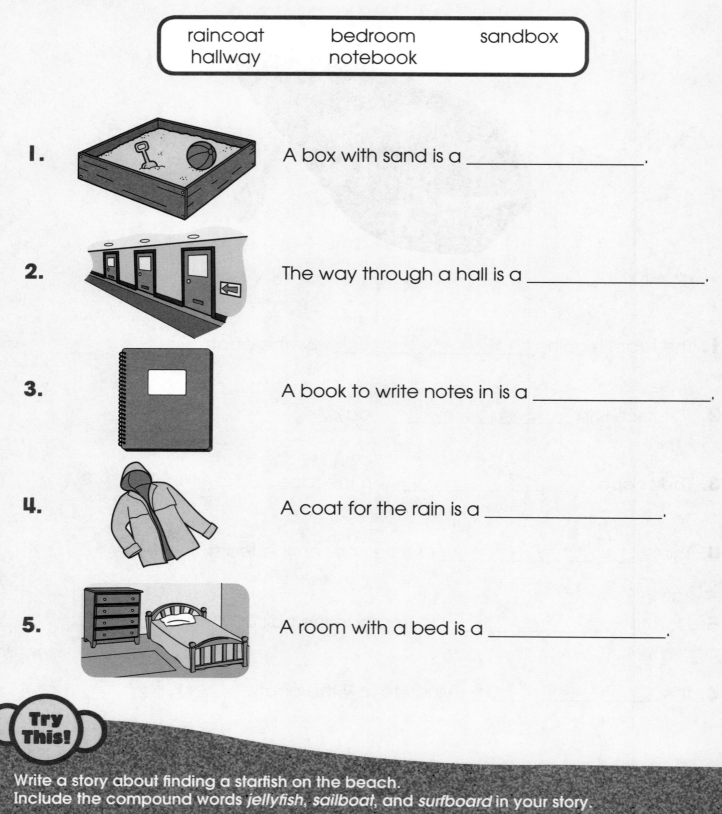

1. A box with sand is a _____.

2. The way through a hall is a _____.

3. A book to write notes in is a _____.

4. A coat for the rain is a _____.

5. A room with a bed is a _____.

Try This!

Write a story about finding a starfish on the beach.
Include the compound words *jellyfish, sailboat,* and *surfboard* in your story.

As Easy as ABC

Directions: Write the words in alphabetical order.

1. _____

2. _____

3. _____

4. _____

hat	cup	ship	boy
goat	lion	apple	truck

5. _____

6. _____

7. _____

8. _____

Try This!

Write three nouns on another sheet of paper.
Find the words in a dictionary. Write the definitions.

In a Pumpkin Patch

Directions: Color each pumpkin fact orange. Color each opinion about pumpkins yellow.

Pumpkin pie is best.

Pumpkins grow on vines.

Pumpkins have seeds.

A pumpkin is a fruit.

Big pumpkins are better.

Pumpkin seeds are tasty.

Try This!

Make a list of 10 things you can do with a pumpkin on another sheet of paper.

Flying High

Directions: Read the story. Answer the questions below.

Learning to Fly

Once, a baby bird was learning to fly. Learning to fly comes naturally to most birds. But, learning to fly was hard for this little bird. He practiced every day. But, still he was not improving.

Getting up in the air was easy. Flying over the trees was no problem. Landing was the tricky part. It seemed he always missed the branch. But, the little bird did not give up. He kept trying and trying. Soon he was flying and landing just like the other birds.

1. How does the little bird feel about learning to fly? _____

_____

_____

2. Write about a time you learned to do something that was hard. _____

_____

_____

Try This!

Write about a bird that you have watched.
What was the bird doing?

Directions: Read about Abraham Lincoln. Then, write about someone else who works or worked hard for peace.

Abraham Lincoln was the 16th president of the United States. When he was president, a war began. People in the North fought against people in the South.

Abraham Lincoln made a famous speech. He said all people were created equal. He wanted all people to live together in peace.

_____

_____

_____

_____

_____

_____

On another sheet of paper, write a poem about peace.

Flying Fish

Directions: Read the passage about flying fish. Answer the questions. Then, read another story about fish on the next page.

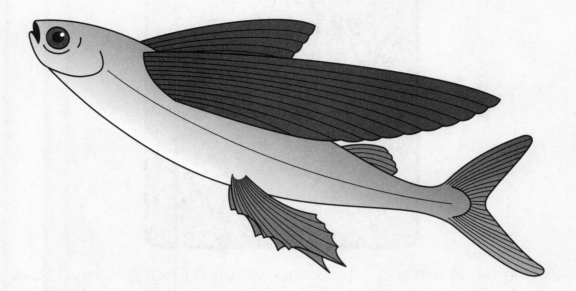

Flying fish do not fly like birds do. A flying fish throws itself from the water with help from its strong tail. Once it is in the air, it spreads large fins. They act like the wings of a glider. They can glide from 150 to 1,000 feet (46 to 305 m) in the air before landing back in the water.

1. Is this passage fiction or nonfiction? _____

2. What is the purpose of this passage? _____

Try This!

How do you think birds and flying fish are alike? How are they different? Make a chart or a Venn diagram on another sheet of paper to explain.

Directions: Read the passage. Then, compare it to the passage you read on page 61.

A little fish in the sea was bored. When a boat passed above her, she jumped into it. "How do you do?" said the fish to the little girl. "Let's have a tea party." The girl and the fish played together. They swam together. They promised to play together every day.

1. Is this passage fiction or nonfiction? _____

2. What is the purpose of this passage? _____

3. If you wanted to learn about fish, which article would you read? _____

_____

Try This!

How are these passages alike and different?

A Tale Too Tall

Directions: Read the tall tale. Underline the parts of the tale that are exaggerations. Then, answer the question.

Grace Chang could make anything grow. If she planted an apple seed, an apple tree would grow by morning. The apples would peel themselves and jump into the nearest pie shell. If she planted cottonseeds, sweaters would spring up overnight. One day, Grace planted a kernel of corn. It grew and grew. People came from all over the state to see it. It grew so big that Grace opened a café inside of it. She served the best corn bread in the state!

How do you know that this story is a tall tale? _____

_____

_____

_____

_____

On another sheet of paper, write a tall tale in which you are the main character. Be sure to exaggerate your talents.

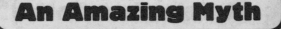

An Amazing Myth

Directions: Read the myth. Then, circle the best title.

Long ago, the animals wanted to plan a surprise party for the king. The dog was the king's best friend. The other animals did not think the dog could keep the secret. So, when they talked about the party, they folded down the dog's ears. This way the dog could not hear the plans. "It's a surprise," they told the dog. The party was a big success. The dog loved being surprised. To this day, many dogs keep their ears down. They are hoping someone is planning a surprise party for them.

"Why Dogs' Ears Hang Down"

"Why Dogs Can Hear Better Than Humans"

"How Dogs Became Pets"

Try This!

On another sheet of paper, write your own myth about an animal. In your myth, explain why the animal is a certain way.

Story Train

Directions: Use the train to plan a story.

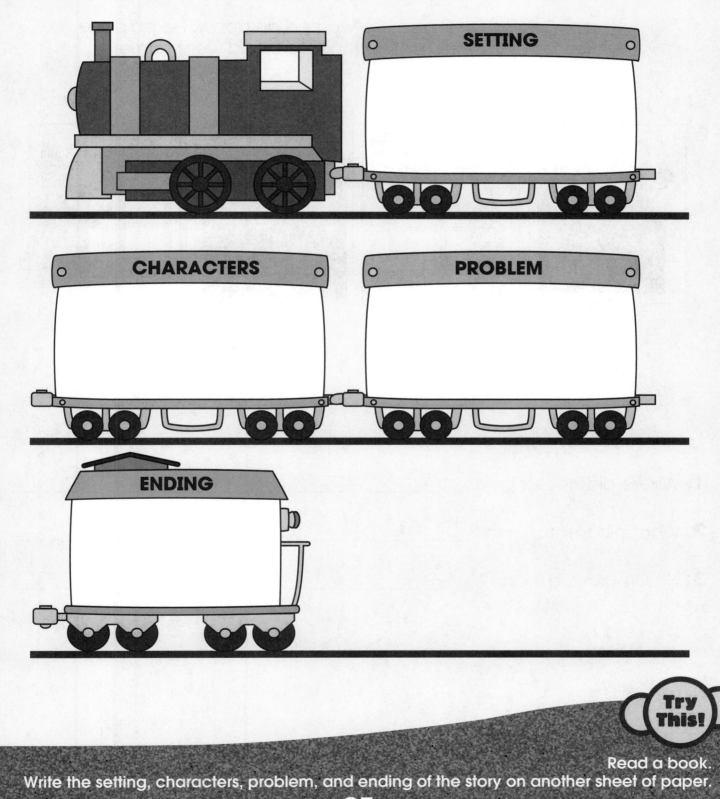

Try This!

Read a book.
Write the setting, characters, problem, and ending of the story on another sheet of paper.

65

And, Then . . .

Directions: Read the story. Number the pictures to show the order of the story. Then, answer the questions.

Hector went to the store. He wanted an apple. He paid the clerk for the apple. Then, he left the store and went home.

1. Where did Hector go? _____

2. What did Hector want? _____

3. How much did it cost? _____

Make a grocery list for breakfast, lunch, and dinner.
Write your list on another sheet of paper.

Flashlight Fish

Directions: Read the story. Number the sentences in the correct order.

What kind of fish comes out only at night? The flashlight fish! It has a special way to stay safe. It has lights under its eyes.

How does the flashlight fish use its lights to stay safe? First, it uncovers its lights by opening its eyelid. Next, it swims in a straight line. A dangerous fish follows the lights. Then, the flashlight fish covers its lights. Last, it turns and races away. The dangerous fish cannot see where the flashlight fish has gone. The flashlight fish is safe.

_____ The flashlight fish covers its lights.

_____ The flashlight fish turns and races away.

_____ The flashlight fish swims in a straight line.

_____ The flashlight fish uncovers its lights.

Try This!

Do you think the flashlight fish is a smart fish? Explain your answer on another sheet of paper.

All About Insects

Directions: Read each paragraph. Then, underline the main idea.

1. All insects have six legs. Butterflies and bees have six legs. They are insects. Spiders have eight legs. They are not insects.

2. Different insects eat different things. Some insects eat plants. Caterpillars eat leaves. Bees and butterflies like the nectar of flowers. Some insects eat other insects. Ladybugs eat aphids.

3. Insects live in different kinds of homes. Bees build hives from wax. Ants and termites build hills on the ground. Some insects like mayflies. Damselflies spend most of their lives underwater. Others live under rocks or in old logs.

Try This!

Some insects protect themselves by blending into their environment. Draw a picture of an insect that can blend into its environment.

Moonwalk

Directions: Read the paragraph. Underline the main idea.

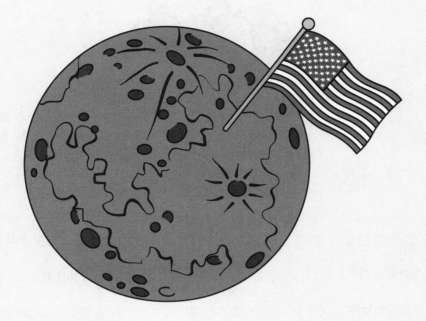

Astronauts Neil Armstrong and Buzz Aldrin were the
first men to walk on the moon. They gathered rocks and
dirt. They left a flag on the moon. They took pictures.
People on Earth saw the pictures on television. They
heard Neil Armstrong say, "That's one small step for man;
one giant leap for mankind." Then, they came back to
Earth in *Apollo 11*. *Apollo 11* splashed into the ocean. The
astronauts were heroes.

Try This!

On another sheet of paper, write at least 10 words using the letters in the word *astronaut*.

An Apple Adventure

Directions: Read the story. Then, follow the directions.

One crisp morning in October, we drove to the mountains to pick apples. We took Daddy's old pickup truck. When we got to the orchard, we spied hundreds of trees filled with apples! Some were golden yellow, and some were bright red. We even saw some that were green. I took a bite from one of the apples. It tasted so sweet. The juice dribbled down my chin. We picked three bushels of apples. Then, we went home to bake some pies.

1. Draw a circle around each word that names a color.

2. Draw a line under a word that means **saw**.

3. Draw a box around the word that tells how the apple tasted.

Try This!

On another sheet of paper, make a list of foods you can make with apples.

The Statue of Liberty

Directions: Read the story. Answer the questions below.

The Statue of Liberty is a symbol of freedom. It was a gift from France. It shows friendship. It is in New York Harbor.

The statue holds a torch. It is in her right hand. She holds a tablet. It is in her left hand. It says *July 4, 1776.*

1. Who gave the Statue of Liberty to America? _____

2. What words are on the tablet? _____

3. Where is the Statue of Liberty located? _____

4. What is the statue a symbol of? _____

Try This!

The Statue of Liberty's crown has seven spikes on it. They represent the continents. Write the name of each continent on another sheet of paper.

Balloons, Balloons!

Directions: Read each sentence. Underline the cause.

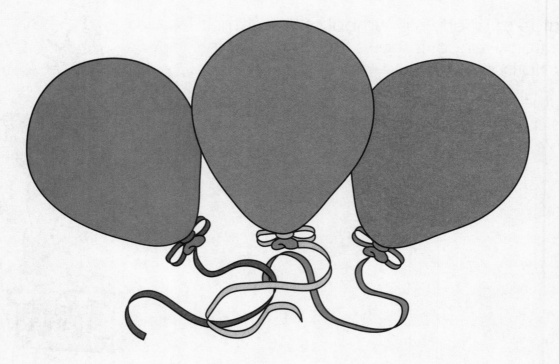

1. The wind blew. The balloons flew high into the sky.

2. Rosa filled the balloons with helium. A balloon popped.

3. My mom bought a balloon. It was my birthday.

4. The children laughed. The clown made silly balloon animals.

5. The balloon flew up. The child let go of the string.

6. The balloon popped. It scared the baby.

On another sheet of paper, write step-by-step directions on how to blow up a balloon.

How Seeds Travel

Directions: Read the paragraph. Then, write the four things that cause seeds to move.

Seeds move from one place to another. Sometimes, people plant seeds. Sometimes, seeds attach to the fur of animals. Sometimes, the wind blows the seeds. Sometimes, seeds float in the water.

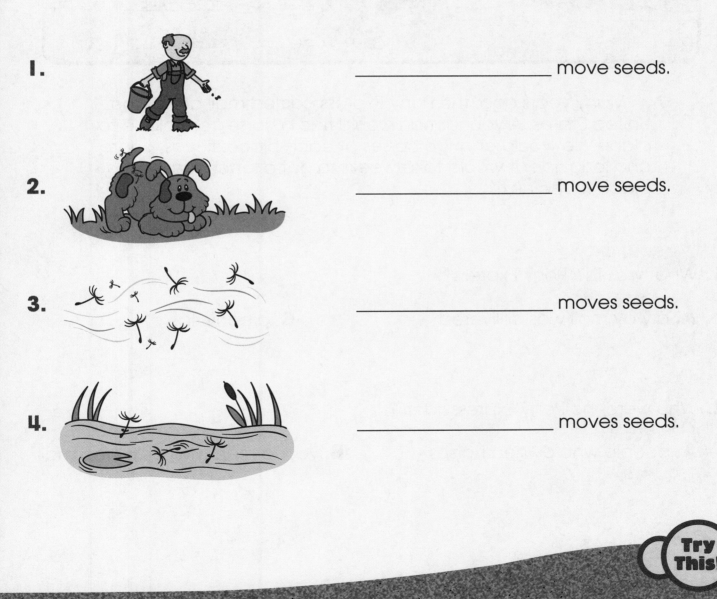

1. _____ move seeds.

2. _____ move seeds.

3. _____ moves seeds.

4. _____ moves seeds.

Try This!

Explain how seeds are carried to different places by animals. Give examples of how this happens on another sheet of paper.

Pony Express

Directions: Read the paragraph. Circle the answer to each question. Then, compare this information to the information on page 75.

Many years ago, the Pony Express carried mail across the United States. A young man would ride a horse from place to place. He would change horses at each place. It was a hard and long ride. It would take weeks to get a letter from one place to the next.

1. What was the Pony Express?

A. a way mail was delivered

B. a pony ride

2. Who were the Pony Express riders?

A. people who owned horses

B. young men who delivered mail

Try This!

Besides letters, list other ways that people communicate. Use another sheet of paper.

U.S. Postal Service

Directions: Read the paragraph. Compare the information to the information on page 74. Answer the question.

Today mail carriers use a truck to deliver mail. Some mail carriers walk. Letters that need to go a long distance travel by airplane. Then, a mail carrier delivers the letter to the correct address. A letter can be delivered in a couple of days. It can even be delivered overnight.

How has mail delivery changed? _____

_____

_____

_____

_____

On another sheet of paper, list the ways that mail delivery today is similar and different from in the past.

Places of Interest

Directions: Draw a line from the sentence to the place of interest each person visited.

I. It was Saturday, so Bailey chose to visit this place.

A.

Open weekdays from 10:00 A.M. to 6:00 P.M. Closed weekends.
Call **555-FISH**

2. Jamie wanted to visit a place where he could learn about dolphins and sharks.

B.

Open Monday – Saturday.
Noon to 6:00 P.M.
Call **555-STAR**

3. Pablo wanted to learn about the United States.

C.

Open Monday – Friday from 9:00 A.M. to 5:00 P.M.
Call **HIS-TORY**

Try This!

Look at the ads above. Which place would you want to visit? Why?
Write about it on another sheet of paper.

Which Tool?

Directions: Read the clues. Draw a line from each clue to its tool.

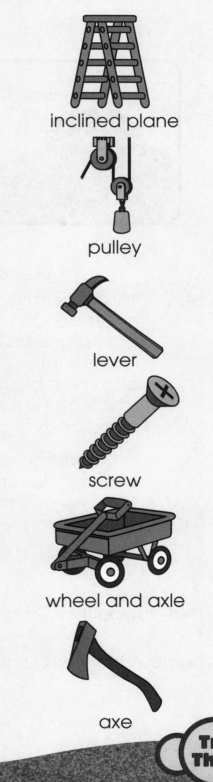

1. What tool can be used to raise a flag up a flagpole?

A.

inclined plane

2. What tool can be used to get a cat out of a tree?

B.

pulley

3. What tool can be used to carry things?

C.

lever

4. What tool can be used to get a nail out of a board?

D.

screw

5. What tool can be used to hang a picture?

E.

wheel and axle

6. What tool can be used to split a log?

F.

axe

Try This!

On another sheet of paper, list other ways to move things from one place to another.

Little Dark Eyes

Directions: Read the story. Answer the questions.

Josh heard something outside in the woods. It was still dark. Ma and Pa were sleeping. Josh lit the candle by his bed. No window was in the little cabin. Josh got up and looked out the front door. Little dark eyes looked back at him. The little dark eyes were part of a great big furry face. Josh saw the eyes rise. He saw that the eyes were part of something tall when it stood on its two legs. "Grrr . . ." growled the eyes.

Slam! Josh shut the door. He put the big wood bar across it. He ran over to the bed and shook his father. "Pa!" he shouted. "Wake up!" He was too scared to say anything else.

1. What do you think Josh saw? _____

2. Underline the words in the story that give clues to what Josh saw.

Finish the story. Use another sheet of paper to write what you think happened next.

Which Seeds?

Directions: Read the clues. Draw a line from the plant to its seed.

1.

The oak tree's seed looks like a small nut.

A.

2.

We eat corn seeds on a cob.

B.

3.

Apple seeds are inside the tree's fruit.

C.

4.

The seeds of a pine tree are in a pinecone.

D.

Try This!

On another sheet of paper, write a story about a seed and how it grew.

Koko Talks

Directions: Read the story. Then, write what the story is about.

Can a gorilla talk? Gorillas do not form words the way humans do. But, one gorilla, Koko, learned sign language. She talked with her hands. And, she understood what humans said.

Dr. Penny Patterson is the scientist who taught sign language to Koko. She showed Koko a picture of the two of them together. Penny pointed to Koko in the picture and asked, "Who's that?"

Koko answered by signing her own name, Koko.

_____

_____

_____

_____

_____

_____

_____

Try This!

With an adult, use the Internet to learn the sign language alphabet. Sign your name for a friend.

A Rainy Day Surprise

Directions: Read the story. Then, write what the story is about.

Sean walked slowly up the steps to the apartment. It was going to be another long, boring afternoon. It was still raining. It had been raining for three days. Puddles were everywhere.

Suddenly, Sean saw something exciting. He saw a spider. Sean loved spiders. And, this one was big and furry. It had been walking up the side of the wall.

Sean knew right away that it was a wolf spider. He studied them in class. All of the rain must have flooded its home. Sean went inside and found his bug cage.

"I will keep it safe until the ground dries out," Sean said to himself. He could hardly wait to call his friend. It would not be a boring day after all.

_____

_____

_____

_____

_____

Try This!

How do spiders help us? Use another sheet of paper to explain.

Take a Guess

Directions: Read each sentence. Write a sentence that tells what you think will happen next.

1. Michelle could not wait to go to the movies. When she got to the theater, she saw a large sign on the door.

_____

2. As Neil was about to get on the bus, he realized he forgot his lunch.

_____

3. The game was tied four to four. Olivia was up next, but she could not find her lucky bat.

_____

Try This!

Use another sheet of paper to tell what you would do if you forgot your lunch for school.

Planting Flowers

Directions: Help Ruby plant her garden. Follow the directions.

1. Start at the arrow. Go right three spaces. Draw a flower in this space.

2. Go down two spaces. Draw a flower in this space.

3. Go left three spaces and down one space. Draw a flower in this space.

4. Go right four spaces and down one space. Draw a flower in this space.

Try This!

On another sheet of paper, list the supplies needed to plant a flower.

Directions: Follow the directions to complete the town.

1. Draw a school by the trees.

2. Draw a flag on a flagpole next to the school.

3. Draw a train on the railroad tracks.

4. Draw two more houses next to the house.

5. Draw a picture of yourself next to the train station.

Try This!

Draw a map of your school on another sheet of paper.
Label at least five important places in your school.

Why Was It Written?

Directions: Read each piece of writing. Circle why it was written.

1.

to inform   to entertain

2.

to inform   to entertain

3.

to inform   to entertain

4.

to entertain   to persuade

Try This!

Locate ads in newspapers or magazines.
Cut them out and glue them on another sheet of paper to make a collage.

Detail Duty

Directions: List an idea you could write about in the center circle. Then, write details you want to share about the idea.

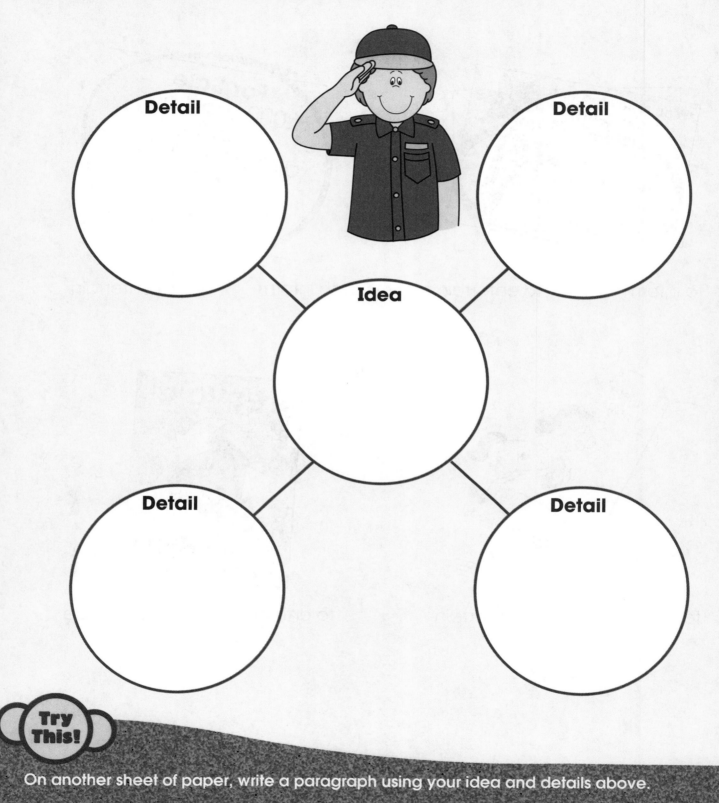

Detail

Detail

Idea

Detail

Detail

Try This!

On another sheet of paper, write a paragraph using your idea and details above.

A Story for the People

Directions: Write a story about the picture. On another sheet of paper, neatly rewrite your story. Check for capital letters and periods.

_____

_____

_____

_____

_____

_____

_____

Why do you think buffalo were important to some American Indians?
Use another sheet of paper to explain your thoughts.

Directions: Finish the sentence about something you believe. Then, write three reasons why.

I believe _____

_____

My reasons are:

1. _____

2. _____

3. _____

Try This!

On another sheet of paper, write a paragraph about what you believe and include your three reasons.

Paragraph Power

Directions: Cross out the sentences that do not belong in the paragraph started below.

Thanksgiving is a special time.

1. It is a time to be thankful.

2. Many families gather for dinner.

3. Many trees lose leaves in the autumn.

4. Some families eat turkey for Thanksgiving dinner.

5. November is the eleventh month.

6. Some people enjoy pumpkin pie.

7. Valentine's Day is celebrated in February.

Try This!

On another sheet of paper, tell how you celebrate Thanksgiving.

A Perfect Paragraph

Directions: A paragraph needs a main idea and a few details. Read the paragraph below and find them in the story. Write them in the chart.

Grizzly bears are huge animals. They may grow up to 8 feet (2.4 m) tall and weigh 800 pounds (363 kg). Their coats can be a creamy brown or black. Their limbs are dark. Their fur is often tipped with white. That is why they are sometimes called *silver tips*.

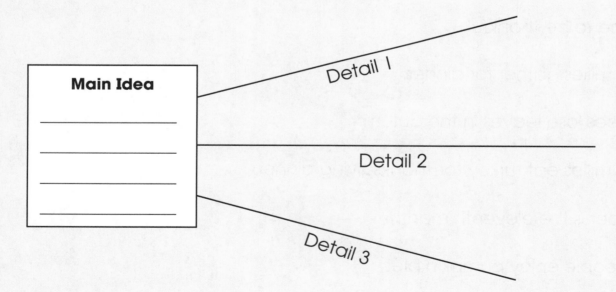

Main Idea

_____

_____

_____

_____

Detail 1

Detail 2

Detail 3

Try This!

Look at a few paragraphs in a book from your library. Can you identify the main idea? Can you name the details? Share with a friend.

Super Speller

Directions: Read the paragraph. Underline the eight misspelled words. Then, rewrite the paragraph without mistakes.

Speling can be hard. It is not eazy to think about spelling each werd right when you are buzy thinking about what to write. That is why it is good to edit yur writin. It is like having a second chanse to do it write.

_____

_____

_____

_____

_____

On another sheet of paper, write five words that you sometimes misspell.

The Five Ws

Directions: Read the story. It is missing a lot of details. Revise the story by writing **who**, **what**, **where**, **why**, and **when** details.

A cat ran in the yard. She saw lots of interesting things in the sky. She wanted to get closer to them, so she climbed a tree. She could not climb back down. The woman called for help. Help arrived, and they saved the cat.

_____

_____

_____

_____

_____

_____

Underline the parts of your revision that show you added *who, what, where, why,* and *when* details.

Growing Rhymes

Directions: Finish each poem with a word that rhymes.

I planted a seed,
In spring it will grow.
Now it is asleep
Under the _____ .

I love to fly
my kite so high.
Where does it fly?
Up in the _____ .

The sand at the beach
is within my reach.
I let the sand
pour through my _____ .

Do you hear the wind blow
through the trees at night?
It makes quite a noise
but stays out of _____ .

Try This!

On another sheet of paper, write words that rhyme with *fly*, *run*, and *day*.

Celebrating Cinquains

Directions: Follow the pattern to write a cinquain.

line 1: a noun

line 2: two words describing the noun

line 3: three **-ing** words describing the noun

line 4: a phrase about the noun

line 5: another word for the noun

Example:

Party

fun, noisy

playing, eating, laughing

time to be together

Celebration

_____

_____

_____

_____

_____

Try This!

On another sheet of paper, write another poem about a celebration.
Share it with a friend.

A Haiku for You

Directions: Follow the pattern to write a haiku poem.

Line 1 has five syllables.

Line 2 has seven syllables.

Line 3 has five syllables.

Example:

Saturday is great.

I play and rest, think and dream.

The weekend is mine.

_____

_____

_____

On another sheet of paper, write another haiku poem.

A Poem About Me

Directions: Write each letter of your name on a different line. Then, write a word that describes you that begins with each letter.

_____

_____

_____

_____

_____

_____

_____

_____

Try This!

This type of poem is called an _acrostic_. On another sheet of paper, write an acrostic poem for someone in your family. Decorate the paper.

Math

36
+ 22

45
+ 11

16
+ 42

82
+ 17

76
+ 22

22
+ 22

41
+ 33

18
+ 60

11
+ 88

30
+ 50

82
+ 13

77
+ 12

76
+ 21

23
+ 66

55
+ 44

26
+ 31

75
+ 21

25¢   10¢   5¢   1¢

Picturing Numbers

Directions: Circle each group of **10**. Write the correct numbers on the lines.

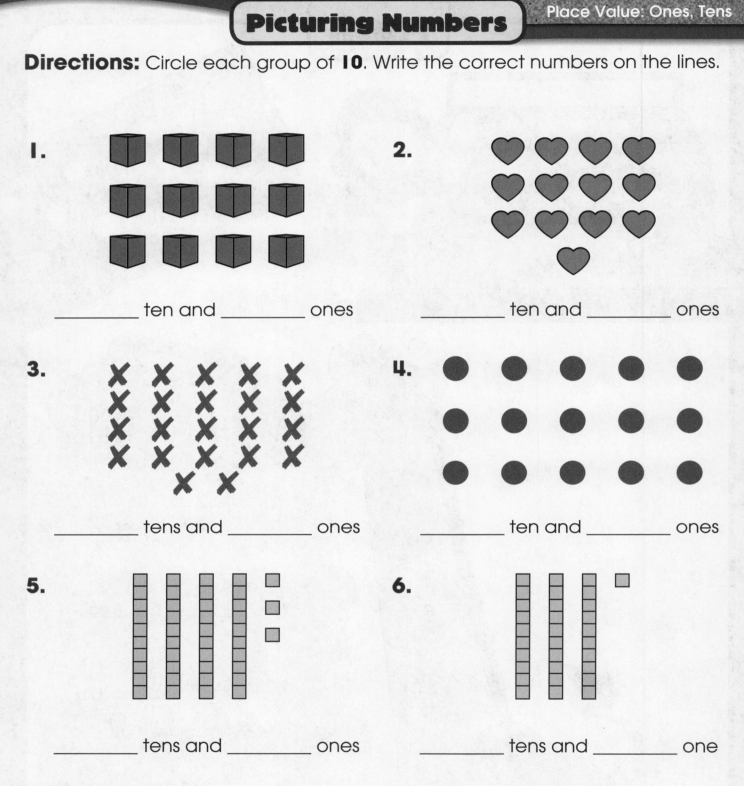

1.

_____ ten and _____ ones

2.

_____ ten and _____ ones

3.

_____ tens and _____ ones

4.

_____ ten and _____ ones

5.

_____ tens and _____ ones

6.

_____ tens and _____ one

Try This!

On another sheet of paper, draw a picture showing the numbers 27, 35, 58, and 77. Group the tens together.

Let's Roll!

Directions: Order the three numbers on the number cubes to make the largest number. Write the number on the line.

1.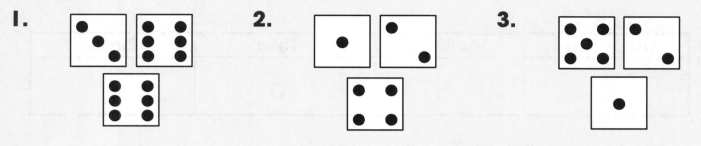

_____

2.

_____

3.

_____

4.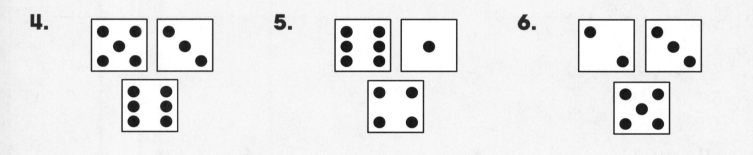

_____

5.

_____

6.

_____

7.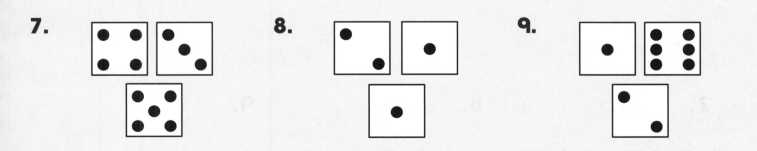

_____

8.

_____

9.

_____

Try This!

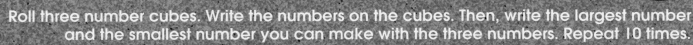

Roll three number cubes. Write the numbers on the cubes. Then, write the largest number and the smallest number you can make with the three numbers. Repeat 10 times.

Place Value: Thousands

Directions: Circle the number in the thousands place. Write its value on the line.

Thousands	Hundreds	Tens	Ones
6	4	3	1

1. 2,456 _____

2. 4,621 _____

3. 3,456 _____

4. 4,286 _____

5. 1,234 _____

6. 5,678 _____

7. 6,321 _____

8. 3,210 _____

9. 7,871 _____

Try This!

Circle all of the numbers in the hundreds place above.

Mix and Match

Directions: Find the equal values. Draw lines connecting them from Column 1 to Column 2 to Column 3.

Column 1	Column 2	Column 3
10 tens	50 ones	60 tens
2 hundreds	30 tens	50
5 tens	6 hundreds	3 hundreds
300	80 ones	20 tens
80	200	100
600 ones	1 hundred	8 tens

Try This!

How many ways can you show or write the number **300**?
Use another sheet of paper.

Stretch It Out

Directions: Match the numbers to their expanded forms.

I.

37

A.

100 + 30 + 6

2.
82

B.
70 + 1

3.
71

C.
30 + 7

4.
136

D.
700 + 40 + 2

5.
742

E.
80 + 2

Try This!

Write five more numbers and their expanded forms on another sheet of paper.

Odd or Even?

Directions: Use a calculator to add or subtract. If the answer is an even number, color the balloon. If it is an odd number, put an **X** on the balloon.

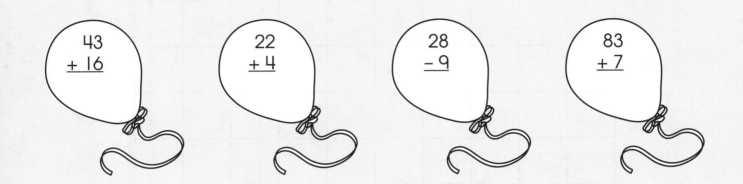

$$43 + 16$$

$$22 + 4$$

$$28 - 9$$

$$83 + 7$$

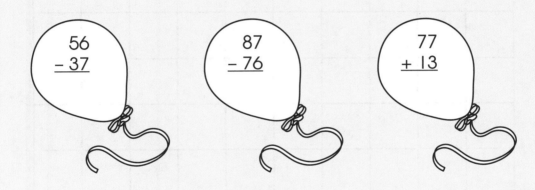

$$56 - 37$$

$$87 - 76$$

$$77 + 13$$

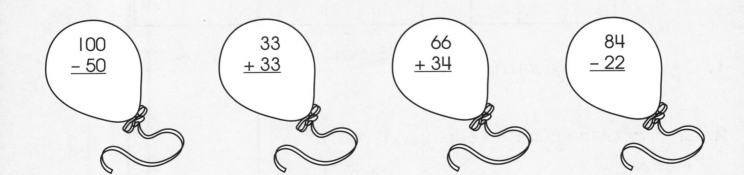

$$100 - 50$$

$$33 + 33$$

$$66 + 34$$

$$84 - 22$$

Try This!

Write the lowest and highest even numbers you can think of on another sheet of paper.

Number Patterns

Directions: Fill in the missing numbers. Look for patterns.

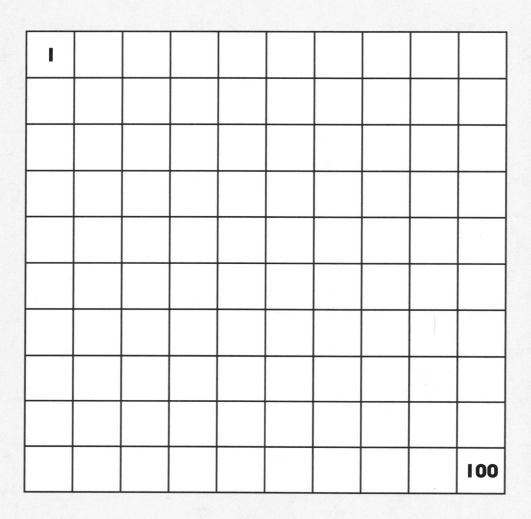

1. Circle all of the even numbers.

2. Color all of the numbers ending in **0** yellow.

3. Draw a green box around all of the numbers ending in **0** or **5**.

On a sheet of grid paper, make another chart starting with **101** and ending with **200**.

104

Buzzing Around

Directions: Write the missing numbers in each row of flowers.

1. 2 4 __ 8 10 __

2. 14 __ 18 20 __ 24

3. 76 78 __ 82 __ __

4. 5 10 15 __ 25 __

5. 45 __ 55 __ 65 __

6. 30 40 50 __ __ __

Try This!

Skip count by 5 from 1 to 100.
Write the numbers on another sheet of paper.

Which Is Greatest?

Directions: Circle the number in each problem that is greatest.

1. 36   52   49

2. 20   19   18

3. 53   61   76

4. 29   27   26

5. 90   98   89

6. 35   43   53

7. 274   261   217

8. 868   888   880

9. 145   194   149

10. 370   363   367

11. 7,000   7,001   6,999

12. 1,203   1,133   1,302

13. 232   334   221   144   322   154

14. 1,002   1,122   2,010   3,100   2,320

On another sheet of paper, write the numbers in problems 13 and 14 from least to greatest.

Laundry Day

Directions: Write each group of numbers in the basket on the shirts from least to greatest.

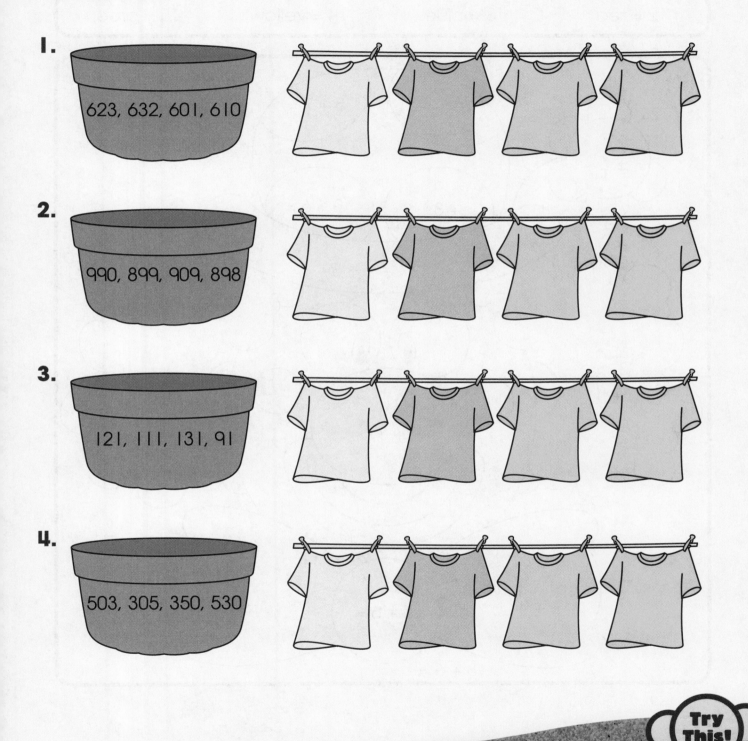

1. 623, 632, 601, 610

2. 990, 899, 909, 898

3. 121, 111, 131, 91

4. 503, 305, 350, 530

Try This!

On another sheet of paper, list reasons why people might hang their clothes outside to dry instead of using a dryer.

Make Them Laugh

Directions: Add. Use the code to color the answers.

12 = red	13 = blue	14 = yellow	15 = green

$6 + 9 =$

$5 + 7 =$

$\begin{array}{r} 7 \\ +\ 7 \\ \hline \end{array}$

$\begin{array}{r} 9 \\ +\ 3 \\ \hline \end{array}$

$9 + 6 =$

$7 + 8 =$

$\begin{array}{r} 8 \\ +\ 4 \\ \hline \end{array}$

$\begin{array}{r} 4 \\ +\ 8 \\ \hline \end{array}$

$\begin{array}{r} 6 \\ +\ 6 \\ \hline \end{array}$

$\begin{array}{r} 9 \\ +\ 4 \\ \hline \end{array}$

$7 + 6 =$

$\begin{array}{r} 5 \\ +\ 8 \\ \hline \end{array}$

$8 + 6 =$

Try This!

Create your own addition picture with a code and have a friend complete it.

Domino Math

Directions: Write the number of dots on each side of the domino. Then, count on to find the sum of both sides. The first one is done for you.

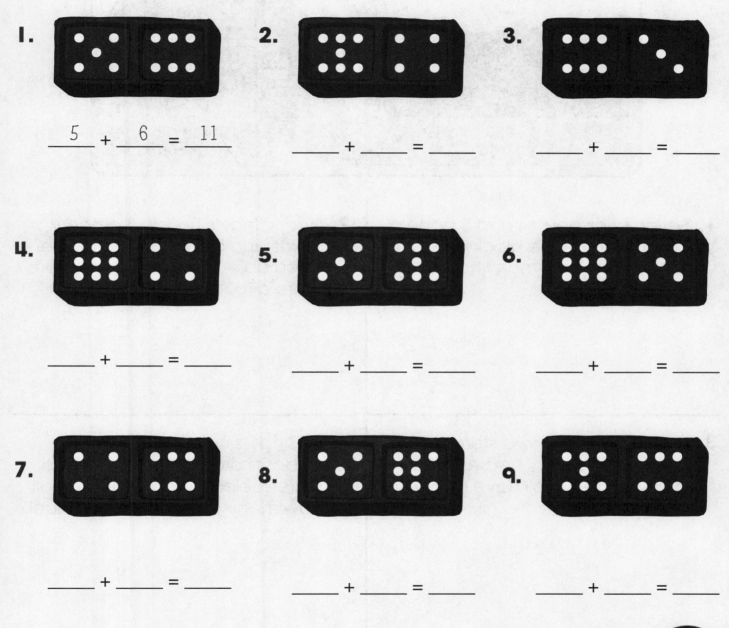

1. __5__ + __6__ = __11__

2. ____ + ____ = ____

3. ____ + ____ = ____

4. ____ + ____ = ____

5. ____ + ____ = ____

6. ____ + ____ = ____

7. ____ + ____ = ____

8. ____ + ____ = ____

9. ____ + ____ = ____

On another sheet of paper, draw 10 more dominoes.
Then, write addition problems to match the dots.

It Adds Up

Directions: Circle the words **in all** or **altogether** and solve the problems.

1. Seven brick houses and 5 stone houses are on the block where Cindy lives. How many houses are there in all?

2. Near Cindy's house, 3 grocery stores and 5 discount stores are open daily. How many stores are there altogether?

3. Children live in 8 two-story houses and in 2 one-story houses. How many houses in all have children living in them?

4. In Cindy's neighborhood, 4 students are in high school and 9 are in elementary school. In all, how many children are in school?

Try This!

On another sheet of paper, write three addition word problems and include the words **in all** or **altogether**.

In the Bag

Directions: Subtract and find the difference for each coin.

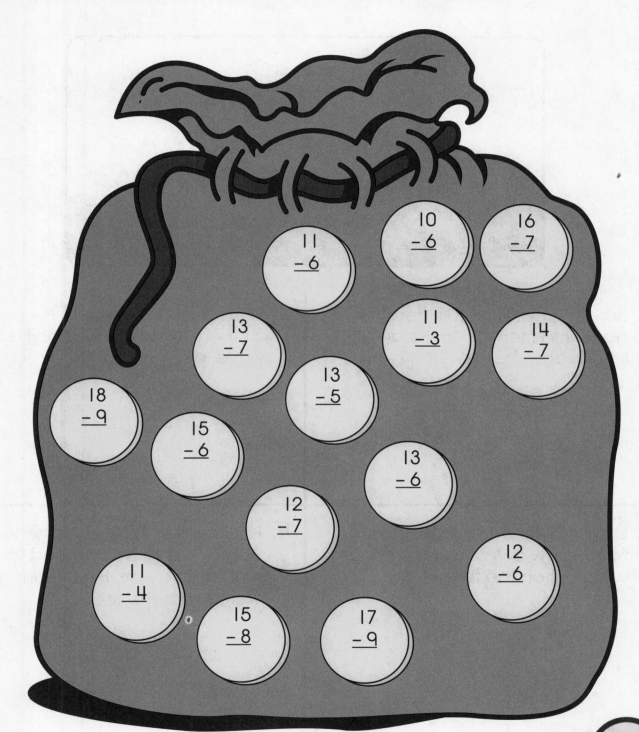

If you add all of the answers together, how much money do you have in the bag?

111

Try This!

Animal Problems

Directions: Read the problems and solve.

1. Barack's cat had 10 kittens. He gave 4 to friends. How many kittens does he have left?

2. Barack had 12 rabbits. He sold 3 of them. How many rabbits did he have left?

3. Eleven birds were on the fence. Seven flew away. How many birds were left on the fence?

4. Fourteen birds were at the feeder. Barack's dog barked and scared 9 of them away. How many birds were still at the feeder?

Try This!

On another sheet of paper, write three addition word problems about Barack and the animals in his yard. Then, solve the problems.

Up, Up, and Away

Directions: Use the numbers in each basket to write a fact family. The first one is done for you.

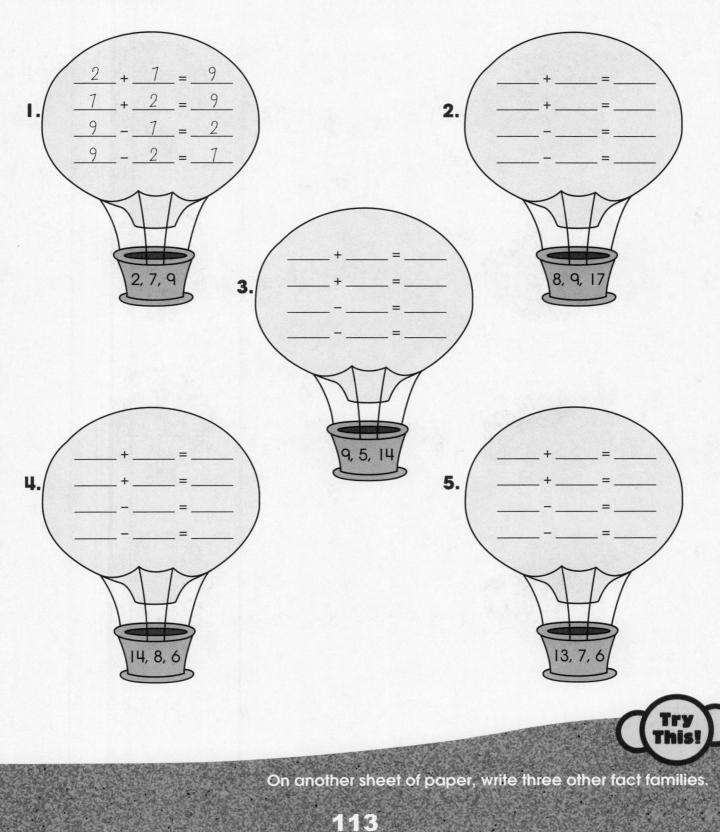

1.
   2 + 7 = 9
   7 + 2 = 9
   9 − 7 = 2
   9 − 2 = 7

   2, 7, 9

2.
   ___ + ___ = ___
   ___ + ___ = ___
   ___ − ___ = ___
   ___ − ___ = ___

   8, 9, 17

3.
   ___ + ___ = ___
   ___ + ___ = ___
   ___ − ___ = ___
   ___ − ___ = ___

   9, 5, 14

4.
   ___ + ___ = ___
   ___ + ___ = ___
   ___ − ___ = ___
   ___ − ___ = ___

   14, 8, 6

5.
   ___ + ___ = ___
   ___ + ___ = ___
   ___ − ___ = ___
   ___ − ___ = ___

   13, 7, 6

Try This!

On another sheet of paper, write three other fact families.

Squirrely Math

Directions: Add or subtract in your head. Then, write the answer on the tree.

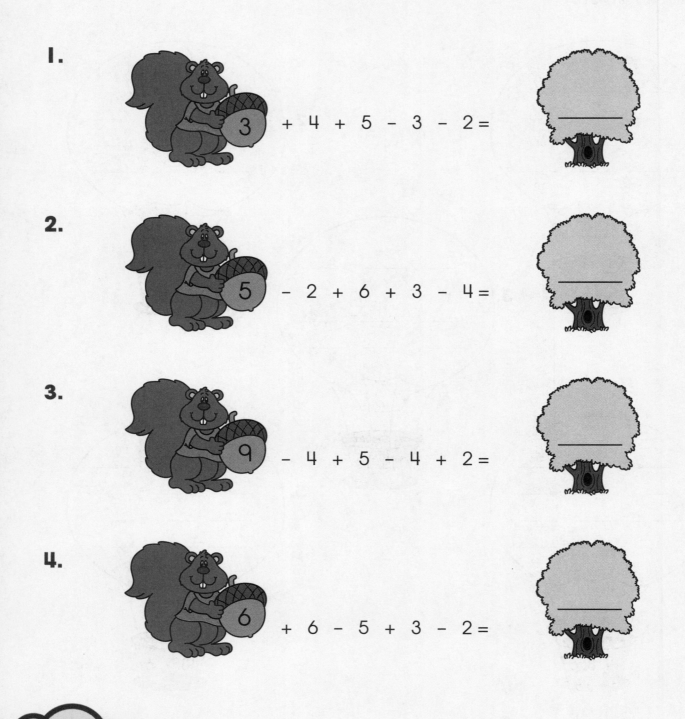

1. 3 + 4 + 5 - 3 - 2 = _____

2. 5 - 2 + 6 + 3 - 4 = _____

3. 9 - 4 + 5 - 4 + 2 = _____

4. 6 + 6 - 5 + 3 - 2 = _____

Try This!

On another sheet of paper, write two more problems like the problems on this page. Then, solve the problems.

Find the Tens

Directions: Circle the two numbers in each math problem that equal 10. Then, add the 10 onto the third number to solve the problem.

1. $2 + 9 + 1 =$ _____

2. $7 + 3 + 3 =$ _____

3. $2 + 9 + 8 =$ _____

4. $5 + 6 + 5 =$ _____

5. $6 + 4 + 1 =$ _____

6. $4 + 6 + 2 =$ _____

7. $8 + 2 + 7 =$ _____

8. $4 + 7 + 6 =$ _____

9. $9 + 9 + 1 =$ _____

10. $4 + 8 + 2 =$ _____

Try This!

On another sheet of paper, choose three problems above and write word problems using the numbers.

In the Park

Directions: Circle either the word **Add** or **Subtract**. Then, write a number sentence and solve each problem.

1. Six swings are in the park. Four children are swinging. How many swings are empty?

Add or Subtract

2. The slide has 8 steps. Craig climbed 3 steps. How many more steps must he climb?

Add or Subtract

3. Ellen went across the monkey bars 5 times. So did Brooke. How many times did both girls go across?

Add or Subtract

4. Three girls sat on a park bench. Three boys sat on another bench. How many children are sitting on benches?

Add or Subtract

Try This!

On another sheet of paper, write two more addition word problems and two more subtraction word problems.

Jumping Contest

Directions: Read the problem and solve.

The frogs were in a jumping contest. Each frog jumped 2 feet shorter than the jump before. How many feet did each frog jump in all? Write each answer on the correct trophy.

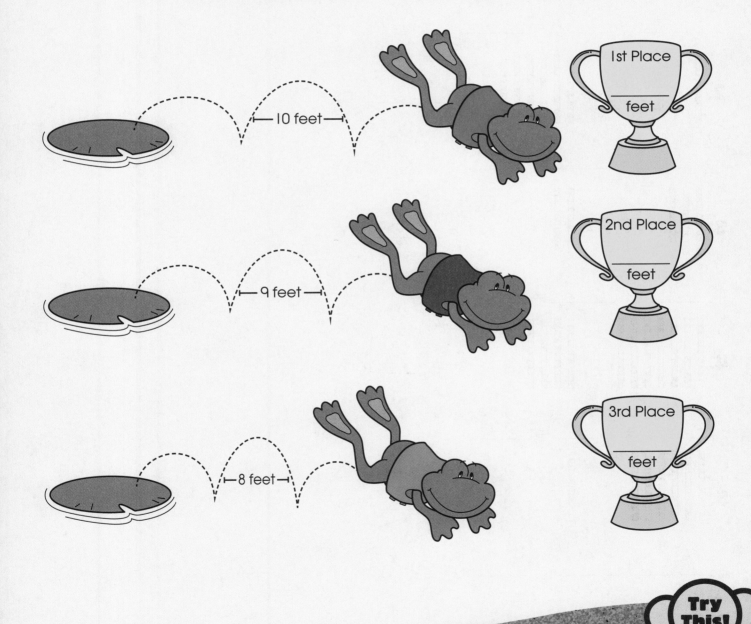

Try This!

On another sheet of paper, write a story about a frog jumping contest.

117

Terrific Tens

Directions: Write how many tens. Then, write the correct addition problem.

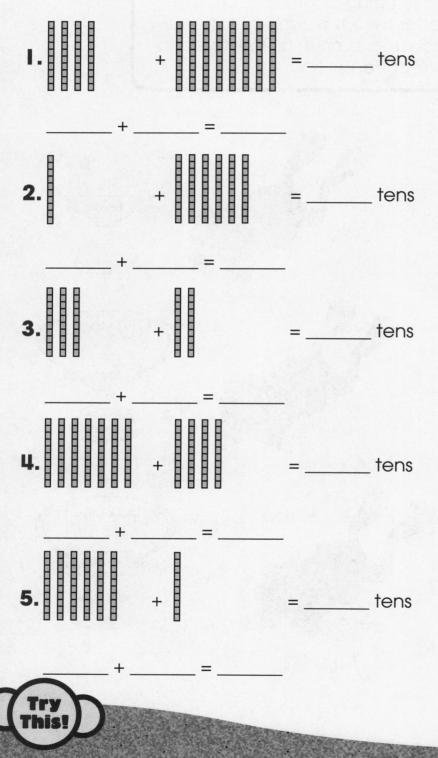

1. ▊▊▊▊▊ + ▊▊▊▊▊▊▊ = _____ tens

_____ + _____ = _____

2. ▊ + ▊▊▊▊▊▊ = _____ tens

_____ + _____ = _____

3. ▊▊▊ + ▊▊ = _____ tens

_____ + _____ = _____

4. ▊▊▊▊▊▊▊▊ + ▊▊▊ = _____ tens

_____ + _____ = _____

5. ▊▊▊▊▊▊ + ▊ = _____ tens

_____ + _____ = _____

Try This!

Turn problems 3, 4, and 5 into subtraction problems. Use another sheet of paper.

Under the Big Top

Directions: Add the ones. Then, add the tens.

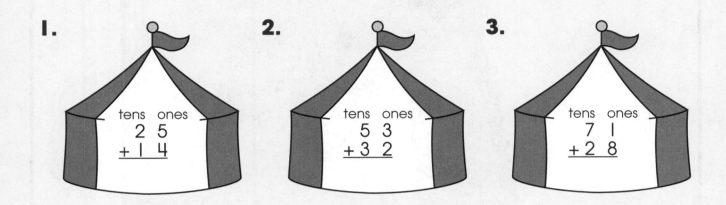

1.
tens	ones
2	5
+ 1	4

2.
tens	ones
5	3
+ 3	2

3.
tens	ones
7	1
+ 2	8

4.
tens	ones
4	4
+ 3	2

5.
tens	ones
5	1
+ 3	7

6.
tens	ones
2	6
+ 5	2

Try This!

Draw base ten blocks to show each of the problems.
Use a line to show a tens block and a dot to show a ones block.

Standing Tall

Directions: Solve each addition problem.

$$36 + 22$$

$$45 + 11$$

$$16 + 42$$

$$82 + 17$$

$$76 + 22$$

$$22 + 22$$

$$41 + 33$$

$$18 + 60$$

$$11 + 88$$

$$30 + 50$$

$$82 + 13$$

$$77 + 12$$

$$76 + 21$$

$$23 + 66$$

$$55 + 44$$

$$26 + 31$$

$$75 + 21$$

Try This!

On another sheet of paper, make a Venn diagram or a chart to tell how giraffes and horses are alike and different.

Cookie Cutters

Directions: Subtract. Circle the answer.

1.
$$\begin{array}{r} 49 \\ -\ 23 \end{array}$$

16   26   25

2.
$$\begin{array}{r} 67 \\ -\ 41 \end{array}$$

26   15   62

3.
$$\begin{array}{r} 58 \\ -\ 37 \end{array}$$

81   11   21

4.
$$\begin{array}{r} 75 \\ -\ 50 \end{array}$$

20   25   35

5.
$$\begin{array}{r} 86 \\ -\ 21 \end{array}$$

67   86   65

6.
$$\begin{array}{r} 64 \\ -\ 52 \end{array}$$

12   26   16

Try This!

On another sheet of paper, write addition problems using the numbers in the problems above. Use a calculator to check your work.

Sail Away

Directions: Solve the subtraction problems.

1.

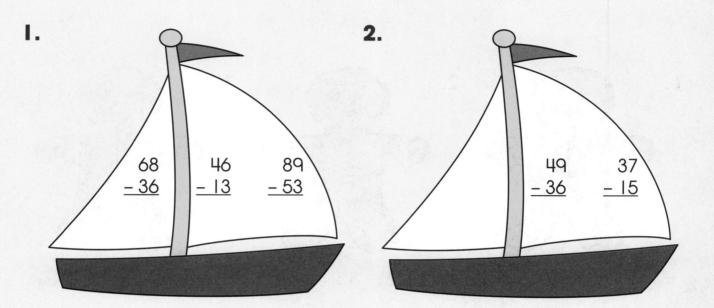

$$68 \atop -36$$ $$46 \atop -13$$ $$89 \atop -53$$

2.

$$49 \atop -36$$ $$37 \atop -15$$

3.

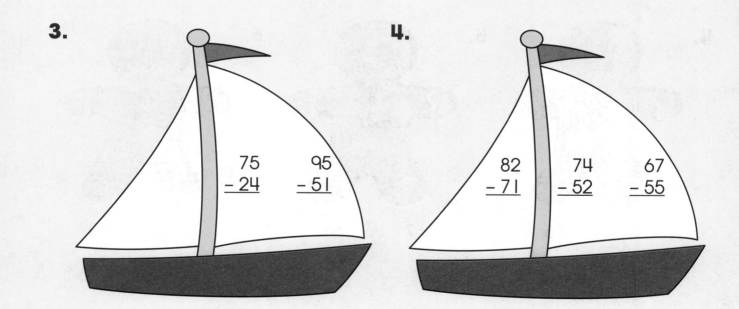

$$75 \atop -24$$ $$95 \atop -51$$

4.

$$82 \atop -71$$ $$74 \atop -52$$ $$67 \atop -55$$

Look at the differences above.
If the difference is even, circle it. If it is odd, cross it out.

On the Farm

Directions: Read the information. Then, answer the questions.

The Johnson's farm has 25 cows, 17 horses, 19 sheep, and 26 hens.

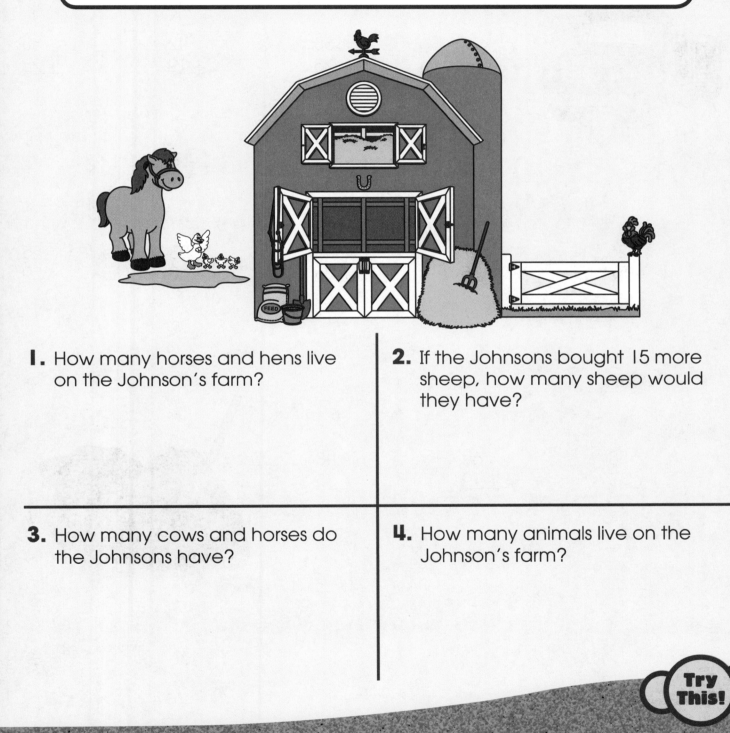

1. How many horses and hens live on the Johnson's farm?

2. If the Johnsons bought 15 more sheep, how many sheep would they have?

3. How many cows and horses do the Johnsons have?

4. How many animals live on the Johnson's farm?

Try This!

Write a story about the Johnson's farm. Include some numbers in your story.

Road Trip

Directions: Write each sum. Connect the sums of **83** to make a road for the truck.

```
  17        58        42        38
+ 66      + 25      + 19      + 25
```

```
  26        17        48        28        65
+ 57      + 75      + 26      + 38      + 29
```

```
  58        64        48
+ 37      + 19      + 35
```

Try This!

When you go on a road trip, you see many signs along the highway.
Draw five signs that you might see along the way.

124

Sea Subtraction

Directions: Fill in each tens and ones chart and solve.

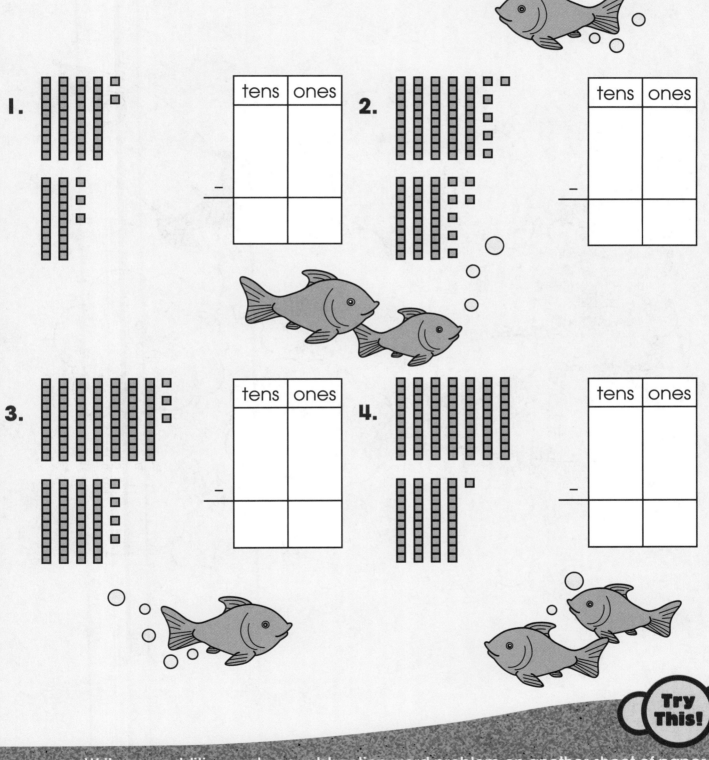

1.

tens	ones
−	

2.

tens	ones
−	

3.

tens	ones
−	

4.

tens	ones
−	

Try This!

Write one addition and one subtraction word problem on another sheet of paper.
Have a friend solve them using base 10 blocks.

125

Blast Off!

Directions: Subtract and solve the problems.

60
− 48

81
− 18

72
− 29

72
− 16

71
− 49

91
− 37

53
− 36

46
− 13

97
− 28

52
− 28

45
− 18

74
− 37

Try This!

Color the clouds of smoke that have the highest and lowest differences.

Money Drawer

Directions: Write the words and values under the correct coin in each drawer.

MONEY BOX

5¢	Ten cents	25¢	Dime
Quarter	Penny	1¢	$0.05
One cent	$0.10	Five cents	Twenty-five cents
10¢	Nickel	$0.25	$0.01

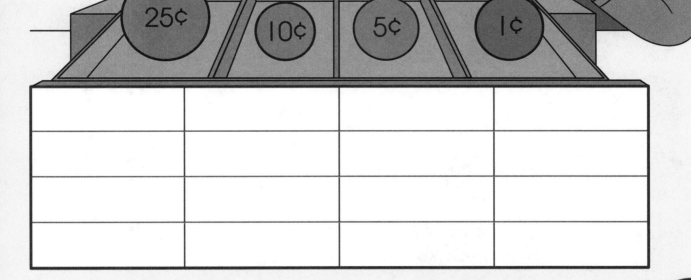

On another sheet of paper, write 10 different combinations of coins that equal $1.00.

Bank on It

Directions: Count the coins. Draw a line to match the coins on the left to their values on the right.

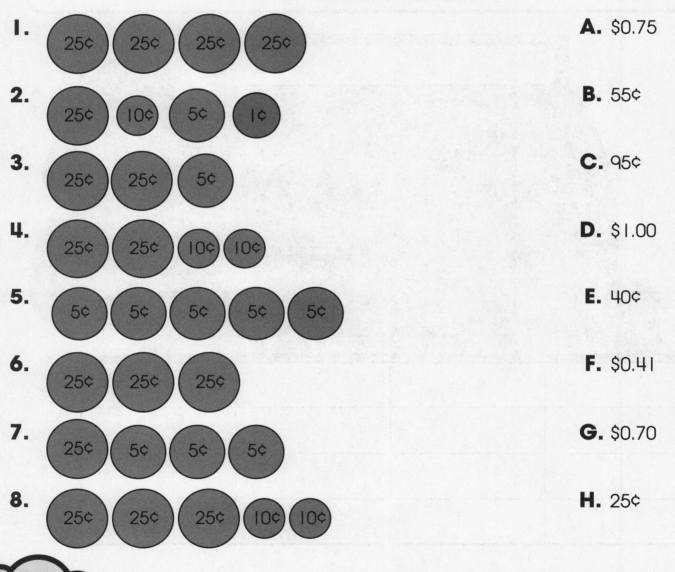

1. 25¢ 25¢ 25¢ 25¢

2. 25¢ 10¢ 5¢ 1¢

3. 25¢ 25¢ 5¢

4. 25¢ 25¢ 10¢ 10¢

5. 5¢ 5¢ 5¢ 5¢ 5¢

6. 25¢ 25¢ 25¢

7. 25¢ 5¢ 5¢ 5¢

8. 25¢ 25¢ 25¢ 10¢ 10¢

A. $0.75

B. 55¢

C. 95¢

D. $1.00

E. 40¢

F. $0.41

G. $0.70

H. 25¢

Try This!

How many different ways can you show $2.00 using coins and bills?
Use another sheet of paper to show at least 10 different ways.

Pocket Change

Directions: Write how much money is in each pocket. Then, draw the same amount using the fewest coins.

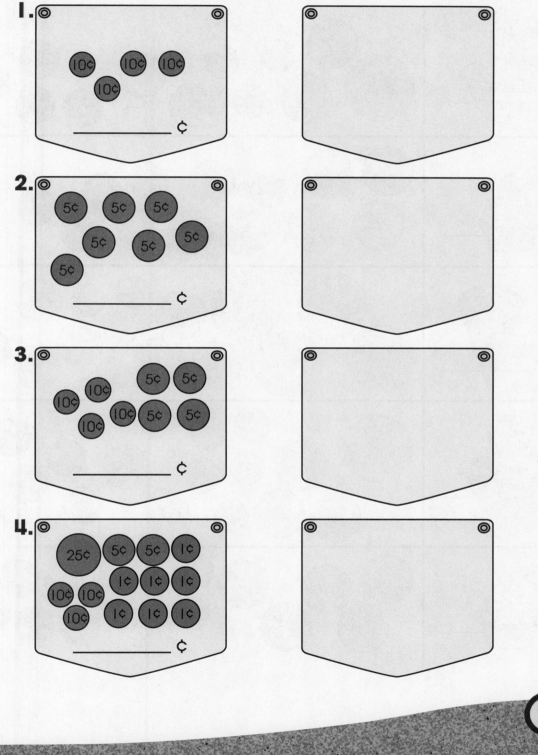

1. 10¢ 10¢ 10¢ 10¢

_____ ¢

2. 5¢ 5¢ 5¢ 5¢ 5¢ 5¢ 5¢

_____ ¢

3. 10¢ 10¢ 5¢ 5¢ 10¢ 5¢ 5¢ 10¢

_____ ¢

4. 25¢ 5¢ 5¢ 1¢ 1¢ 1¢ 1¢ 10¢ 10¢ 1¢ 1¢ 1¢ 10¢

_____ ¢

Try This!

Count all of the money in numbers 1 through 4. Write the total amount.

129

Yogurt Shop

Directions: Cross out the coins needed to buy each yogurt treat.

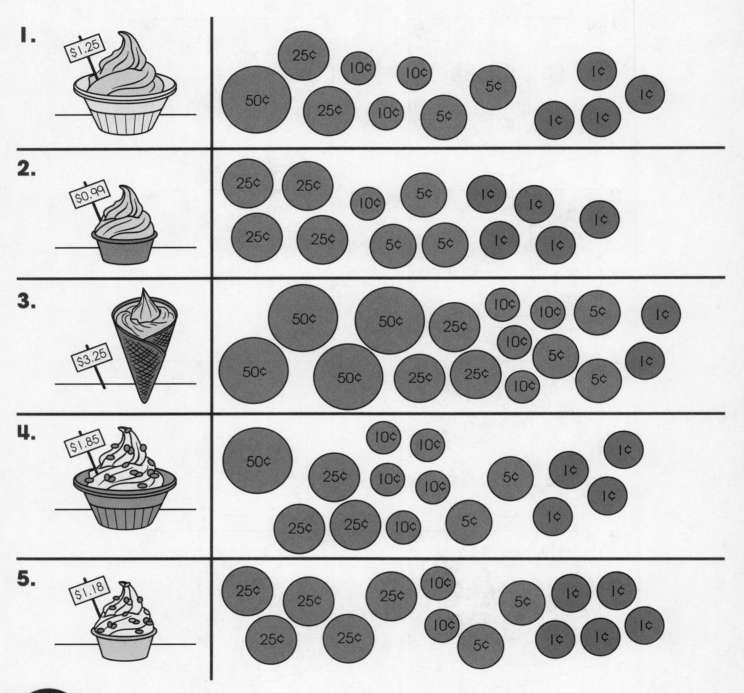

1. $1.25 — 50¢, 25¢, 25¢, 10¢, 10¢, 10¢, 10¢, 5¢, 5¢, 1¢, 1¢, 1¢, 1¢, 1¢

2. $0.99 — 25¢, 25¢, 25¢, 25¢, 10¢, 5¢, 5¢, 5¢, 1¢, 1¢, 1¢, 1¢, 1¢

3. $3.25 — 50¢, 50¢, 50¢, 50¢, 25¢, 25¢, 25¢, 10¢, 10¢, 10¢, 10¢, 5¢, 5¢, 5¢, 5¢, 1¢, 1¢

4. $1.85 — 50¢, 25¢, 25¢, 25¢, 10¢, 10¢, 10¢, 10¢, 10¢, 5¢, 5¢, 1¢, 1¢, 1¢, 1¢

5. $1.18 — 25¢, 25¢, 25¢, 25¢, 25¢, 10¢, 10¢, 5¢, 5¢, 1¢, 1¢, 1¢, 1¢, 1¢

Try This!

If you had $4.00, which yogurt treat would you buy?
How much change would you get back? Show your work on another sheet of paper.

Add It Up!

Directions: Count the money amounts and write each amount as a decimal. Then, add the money together to find the total amount.

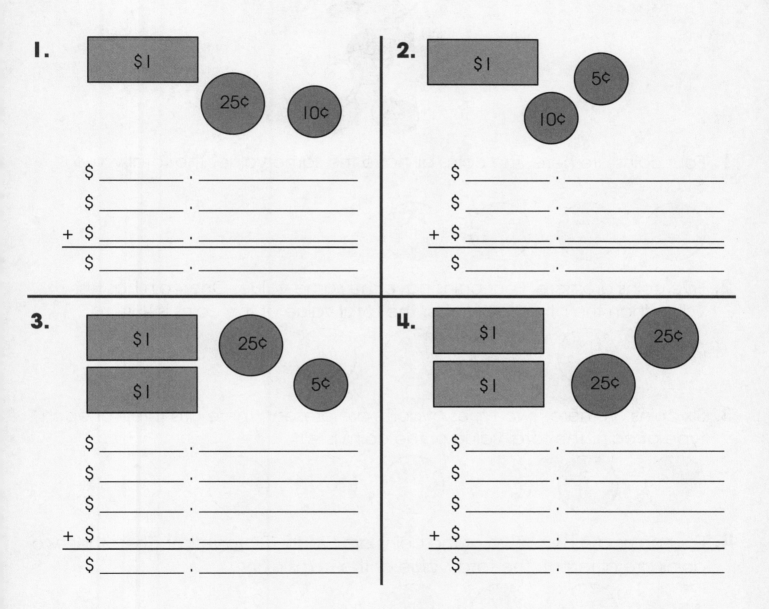

1.

$1   25¢   10¢

$ _____ . _____

$ _____ . _____

+ $ _____ . _____

$ _____ . _____

2.

$1   5¢   10¢

$ _____ . _____

$ _____ . _____

+ $ _____ . _____

$ _____ . _____

3.

$1   25¢ $1   5¢

$ _____ . _____

$ _____ . _____

$ _____ . _____

+ $ _____ . _____

$ _____ . _____

4.

$1   25¢ $1   25¢

$ _____ . _____

$ _____ . _____

$ _____ . _____

+ $ _____ . _____

$ _____ . _____

Try This!

On another sheet of paper, write a word problem about one of the problems above.

Mystery Money

Directions: Read the problems. Write the value of each coin in the correct circle.

I. Four coins are here. The coins all have the same value. The total value is $1.00.

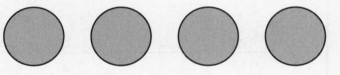

2. Five coins are here. Four coins have the same value. One coin has less value than the other four coins. The total value of the coins is 45¢.

3. Six coins are here. Two types of coins are present. There are three of each type of coin. The total value of the coins is 90¢.

4. Four coins are here. Two of the coins are worth 10¢ together. The other two coins are different. The total value of the coins is 36¢.

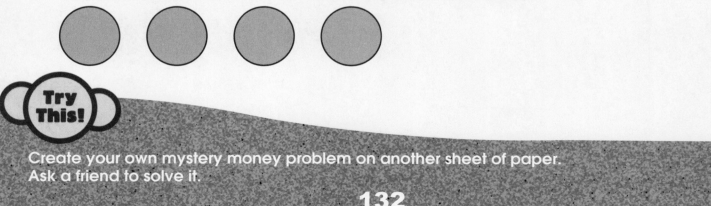

Try This!

Create your own mystery money problem on another sheet of paper. Ask a friend to solve it.

Draw and Solve

Example:

Draw 2 groups of 3 apples.

$3 + 3 = 6$

or $2 \times 3 = 6$

1. Draw 3 groups of 4 hearts.

$4 + 4 + 4 =$ _____

or $3 \times$ _____ $=$ _____

2. Draw 2 groups of 5 boxes.

$5 +$ _____ $=$ _____

or $2 \times$ _____ $=$ _____

3. Draw 6 groups of 2 circles.

$2 +$ _____ $+$ _____ $+$ _____ $+$ _____ $+$ _____ $=$ _____

or $6 \times$ _____ $=$ _____

4. Draw 7 groups of 3 triangles.

$3 +$ _____ $+$ _____ $+$ _____ $+$ _____ $+$ _____ $+$ _____ $=$ _____

or $7 \times$ _____ $=$ _____

Try This!

On another sheet of paper, draw 5 groups of 5 pencils. Solve.

Cookie Factory

Directions: Draw a line from each set of cookies to the number sentence that shows how many chocolate chips.

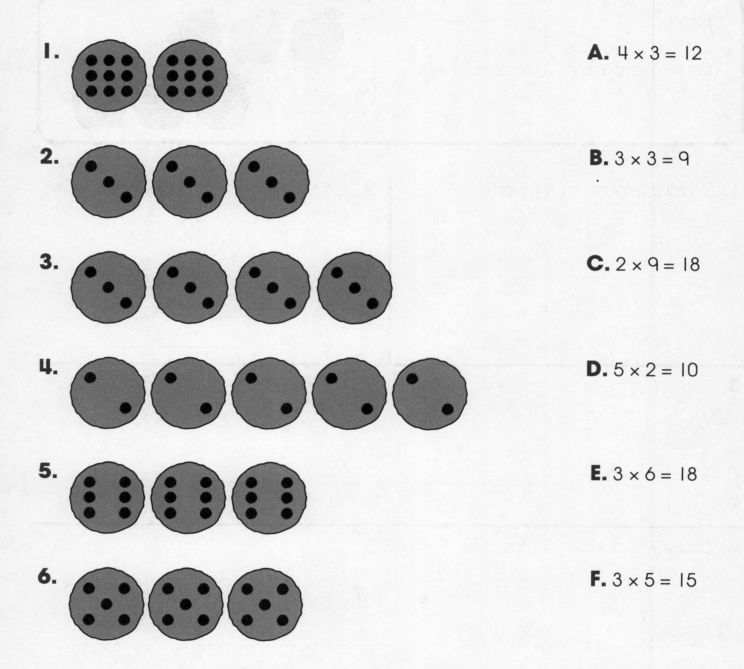

1.

2.

3.

4.

5.

6.

A. $4 \times 3 = 12$

B. $3 \times 3 = 9$

C. $2 \times 9 = 18$

D. $5 \times 2 = 10$

E. $3 \times 6 = 18$

F. $3 \times 5 = 15$

Try This!

Twelve are in a dozen. How many cookies would you have if you baked 3 dozen cookies? Draw a picture on another sheet of paper to show your thinking.

Shine On

Directions: Multiply. Use the key to color each section.

20 = yellow	16 = blue	6 = red
12 = purple	30 = green	24 = orange

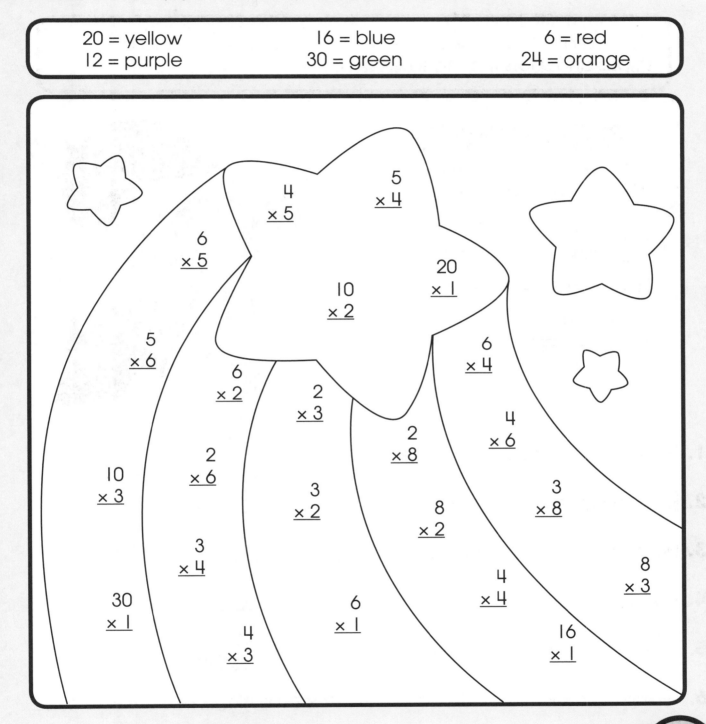

Write a multiplication word problem about a star on another sheet of paper.

Try This!

135

On a Safari

Directions: Read the information. Then, answer the questions.

On a safari, Derek saw many animals. He made a record of the stripes and spots that he saw.

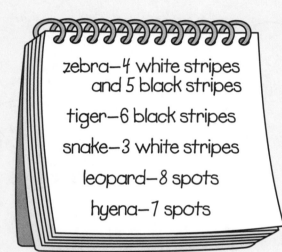

zebra—4 white stripes and 5 black stripes

tiger—6 black stripes

snake—3 white stripes

leopard—8 spots

hyena—7 spots

1. How many stripes are on 6 tigers? _____

2. How many spots are on 9 leopards? _____

3. How many stripes are on 7 snakes? _____

4. How many spots are on 7 hyenas? _____

5. How many stripes are on 8 zebras? _____

6. Which has more black stripes: 3 tigers or 4 zebras? _____

On another sheet of paper, draw pictures to show the problems above.

Planting Flowers

Directions: Read each problem. Draw a picture to solve it. Then, complete the number sentence.

1. 10 flowers

2 flowerpots

How many are in each pot?

10 ÷ 2 = _____

2. 12 flowers

3 flowerpots

How many are in each pot?

12 ÷ 3 = _____

3. 8 flowers

2 flowers in each pot

How many pots?

8 ÷ 2 = _____

4. 15 flowers

3 flowers in each pot

How many pots?

15 ÷ 3 = _____

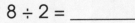
Try This!

Multiplication and division have fact families, too!
Write fact families using multiplication and division for each problem.

Bake a Cake

Directions: Solve each division problem. Draw pictures to help you. Write the division problem and circle the answer.

1. Lin must make 6 cakes for the party. She needs 24 eggs. Each cake needs the same amount of eggs. How many eggs will each cake need?

2. Lin has 18 stars to decorate the cakes. How many stars will each cake have?

3. Lin wants all 54 people at the party to have a piece of cake. How many slices should there be for each cake?

Try This!

If Lin had to make 12 cakes, how many eggs would she need?

Multiply or Divide?

Directions: Read each problem. Draw a picture to solve it. Then, write the number sentence.

1. Thirty-six books are on 4 shelves. Each shelf has the same number of books on it. How many books are on each shelf?

_____ □ _____ = _____ books

2. Logan's dad is paying for Logan and his 3 friends to go to the movies. The tickets cost $8 each. How much money is needed for Logan, his dad, and his 3 friends to go?

_____ □ _____ = $ _____

3. Six baskets are in the room. Each basket has 5 apples in it. How many apples are there in all?

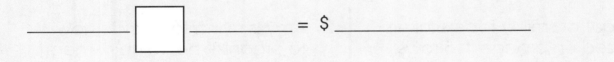

_____ □ _____ = _____ apples

4. A clown at a party has 24 balloons. Six children are at the party. How many balloons will each child get?

_____ □ _____ = _____ balloons

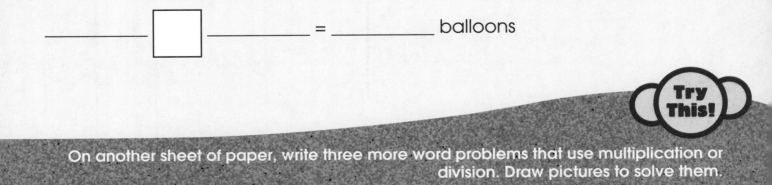

Try This!

On another sheet of paper, write three more word problems that use multiplication or division. Draw pictures to solve them.

Collecting Stickers

Directions: Read the information. Solve each word problem.

> Amy collects stickers. She has 25 smiley faces, 35 sparkly stars, 15 scratch-and-sniff, 30 rainbow hearts, and 20 teddy bears.

1. Amy has her smiley face stickers organized on a page in 5 rows. How many stickers does she have in each row?

2. Amy is trying to decide how to organize her rainbow heart stickers. Show two ways she could organize her stickers.

3. Amy bought 7 packages of stickers. Each package has 6 stickers. How many stickers did Amy buy?

4. How many stickers does Amy have altogether including the stickers she just bought?

On another sheet of paper, draw one of Amy's groups of stickers. Organize them in equal rows on the paper.

Laying Eggs

Directions: Each egg equals 5. Solve the problems.

1. 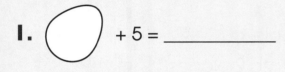 + 5 = _____

2. 21 + 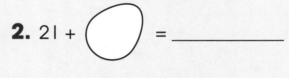 = _____

3. 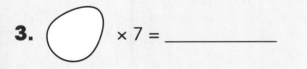 × 7 = _____

4. 30 ÷ 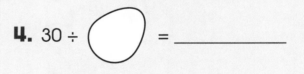 = _____

5. 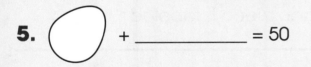 + _____ = 50

6. 100 – 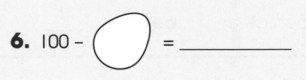 = _____

7. _____ – 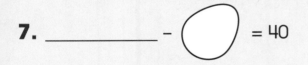 = 40

8. _____ ÷ 9 =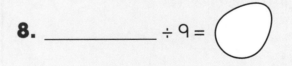

9. 48 – 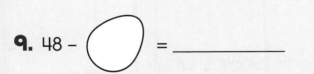 = _____

10. 20 ÷ 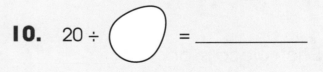 = _____

Try This!

On another sheet of paper, solve all of the problems with each egg equaling 2.

Figuring Out Fractions

Directions: Read each problem. Draw a picture to solve it. Then, complete the sentence.

1. I pie

Cut into 8 slices

Each piece is labeled _____.

2. I apple

Cut into 2 pieces

Each piece is labeled _____.

3. I tray of brownies

Cut into 16 pieces

Each piece is labeled _____.

4. I sandwich

Cut into 4 pieces

Each piece is labeled _____.

Try This!

On another sheet of paper, show how you can divide a pizza equally into 3, 4, 5, and 10 slices.

Fraction Food

Directions: Count the equal parts. Circle the fraction that names one of the parts.

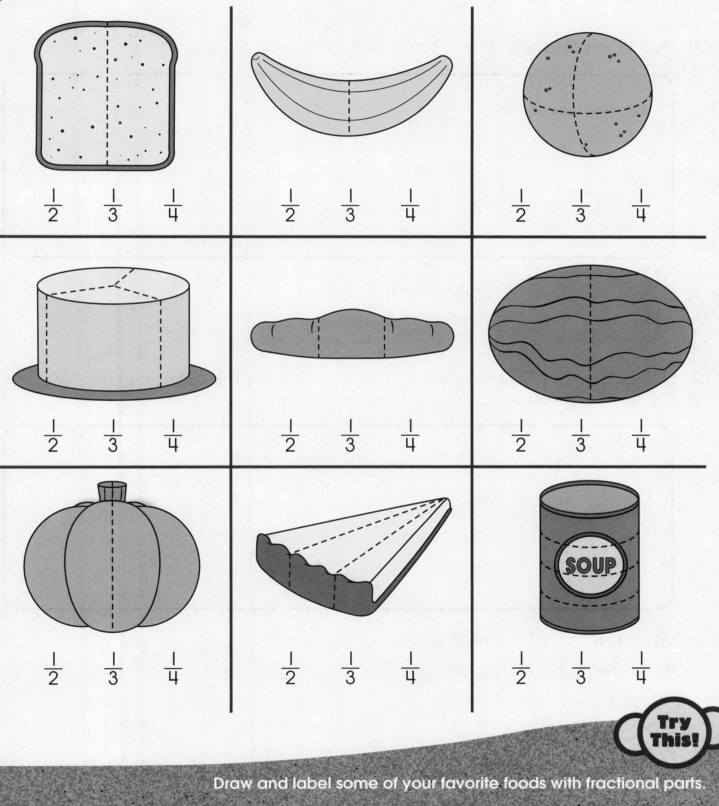

$\frac{1}{2}$ $\frac{1}{3}$ $\frac{1}{4}$ $\frac{1}{2}$ $\frac{1}{3}$ $\frac{1}{4}$ $\frac{1}{2}$ $\frac{1}{3}$ $\frac{1}{4}$

$\frac{1}{2}$ $\frac{1}{3}$ $\frac{1}{4}$ $\frac{1}{2}$ $\frac{1}{3}$ $\frac{1}{4}$ $\frac{1}{2}$ $\frac{1}{3}$ $\frac{1}{4}$

$\frac{1}{2}$ $\frac{1}{3}$ $\frac{1}{4}$ $\frac{1}{2}$ $\frac{1}{3}$ $\frac{1}{4}$ $\frac{1}{2}$ $\frac{1}{3}$ $\frac{1}{4}$

Try This!

Draw and label some of your favorite foods with fractional parts.

Fluttering Fractions

Directions: Draw a picture of each word problem. Then, answer the questions.

1. Four butterflies are on a bush. One is pink. The rest are orange.

What fraction of the butterflies is pink? _____

What fraction of the butterflies is orange? _____

2. Five birds are eating at the bird feeder. Three of the birds are blue. Two of the birds are red.

What fraction of the birds is blue? _____

What fraction of the birds is red? _____

Try This!

Write two new word problems like the ones above. Draw a picture of each word problem. Then, write fractions that tell about the word problems.

Directions: Draw a picture to solve each problem.

1. Jason has 36 pictures in a photo album. One-third of the pictures are of his family. How many pictures are of his family?

2. Fiona has 90 pictures of her friends. One-half of the pictures are of boys. How many of Fiona's pictures are of boys?

3. Emily's album has 28 pictures in it. One-fourth of the pictures are of her baby brother. How many pictures does she have of her baby brother?

4. Carla has 35 pictures in her album. She has one-fifth of her pictures on each page. How many pictures does she have on each page?

On another sheet of paper, draw a picture to show how you would organize 20 pictures in an album.

I Spy Shapes

Directions: Count the shapes in the picture. Write the number of each shape.

_____ circles   _____ rectangles   _____ triangles

_____ squares   _____ rhombuses   _____ ovals

Try This!

On another sheet of paper, draw a scene from a park using only the shapes you see here.

The Race Is On

Directions: Follow the directions.

1. Draw a car that has no edges.

2. Draw a car that has four circles, a rectangle, two triangles, and three squares.

3. Draw a car that uses ovals, circles, and trapezoids.

4. Draw a car without any curves.

Use a ruler to make your own shape car on another sheet of paper.

Taking Shape

Directions: Solve each problem.

1. Draw a plus sign in the center of each shape from edge to edge. Then, circle the shapes that have four identical shapes.

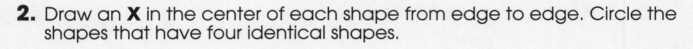

2. Draw an **X** in the center of each shape from edge to edge. Circle the shapes that have four identical shapes.

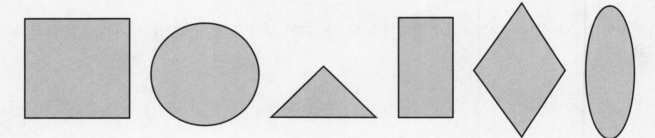

3. Circle the two shapes that are made by dividing the square into halves in two different ways.

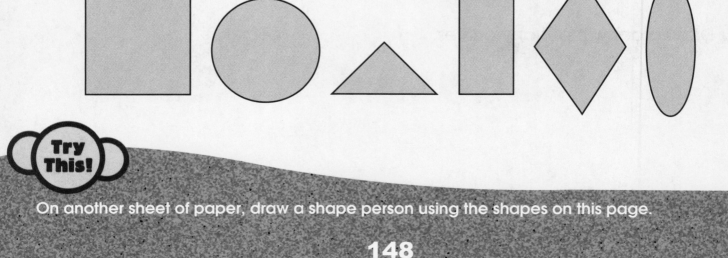

Try This!

On another sheet of paper, draw a shape person using the shapes on this page.

Everything's the Same

Directions: Circle each pair of congruent figures. Cross out each pair that is not congruent.

1.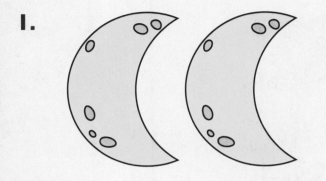

2.

3.

4.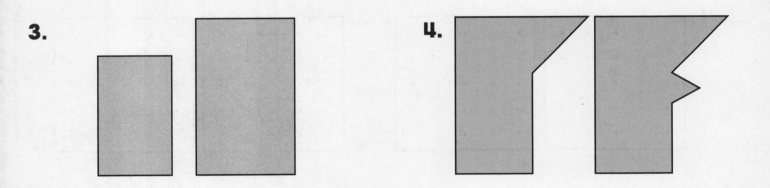

5.

6.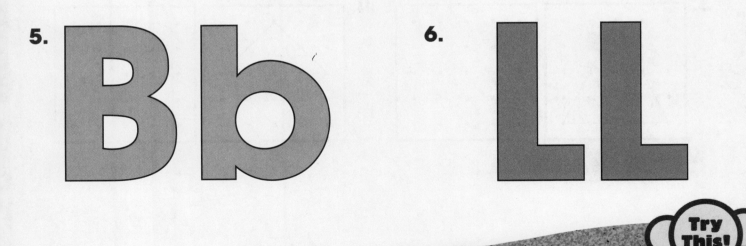

Try This!

On another sheet of paper, draw three more sets of congruent figures and three more sets of figures that are not congruent.

149

Copycat

Directions: Draw a figure to match each figure shown.

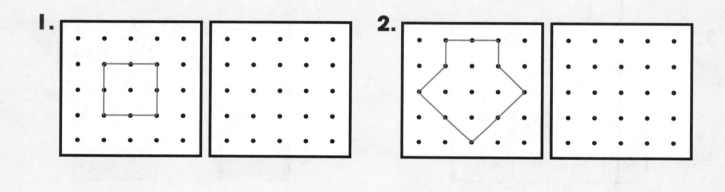

1.

2.

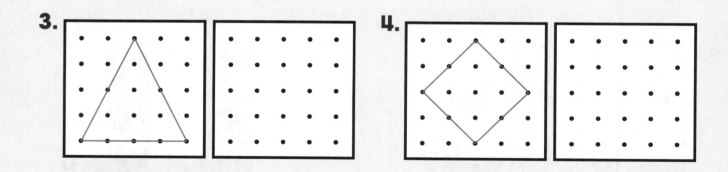

3.

4.

Try This!

Draw two 5 x 5 geoboards on another sheet of paper.
Draw the smallest and the largest squares that can be made on each board.

Fancy Figures

Directions: Look at the pair of figures in each box. Circle whether the figures show a flip, a slide, or a turn

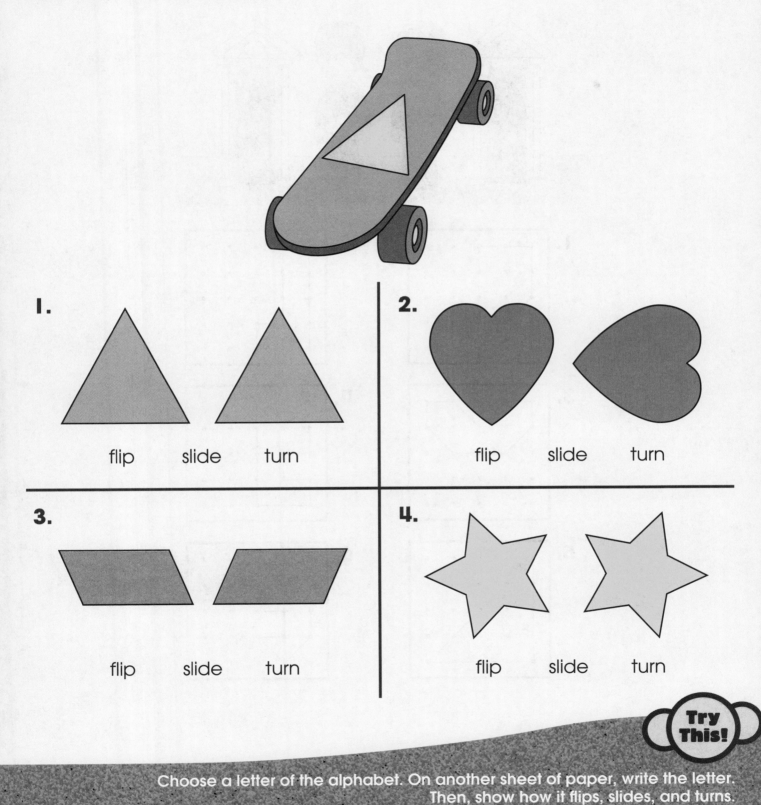

1.

flip   slide   turn

2.

flip   slide   turn

3.

flip   slide   turn

4.

flip   slide   turn

Try This!

Choose a letter of the alphabet. On another sheet of paper, write the letter. Then, show how it flips, slides, and turns.

Geoboard Symmetry

Directions: Finish the figures. Make each figure symmetrical.

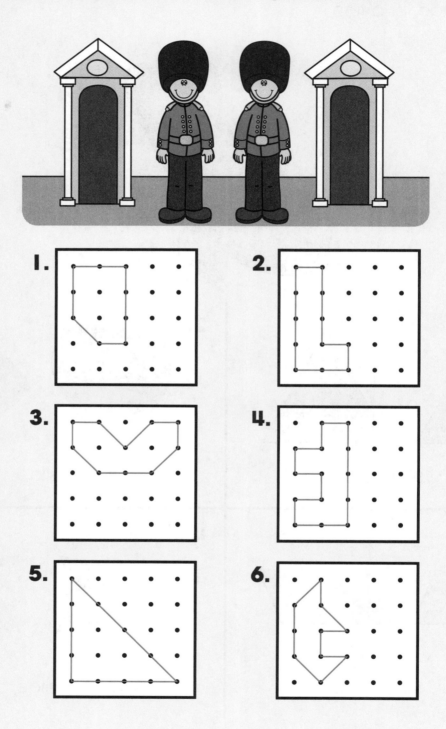

1.
2.
3.
4.
5.
6.

Try This!

Cut a picture from a magazine. Cut the picture in half.
Glue half of the picture onto another sheet of paper. Draw the other half.

Solid Match

Directions: Draw a line from each solid to its name.

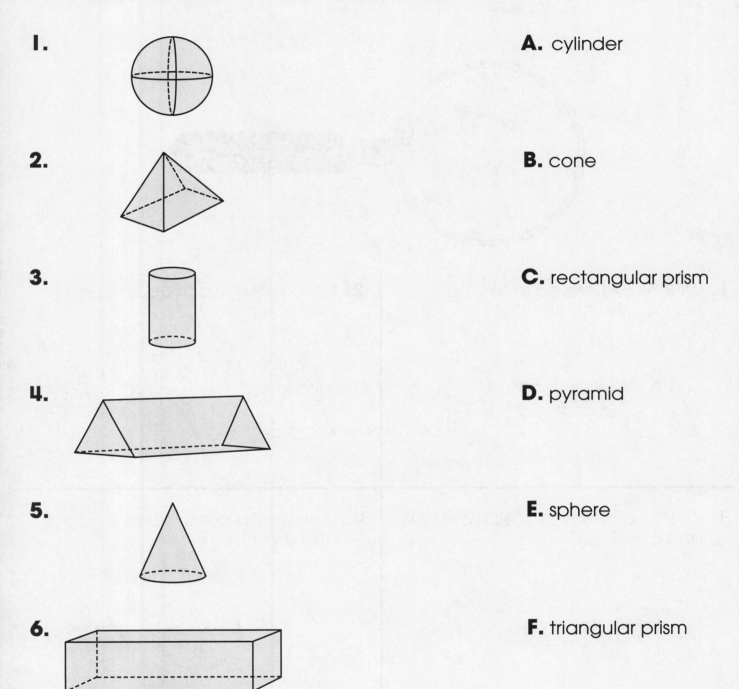

1.

2.

3.

4.

5.

6.

A. cylinder

B. cone

C. rectangular prism

D. pyramid

E. sphere

F. triangular prism

Look around the room and find three solids.
Draw these solids on another sheet of paper.

Solid Clues

Directions: Read the clues. Circle each solid that matches the clues.

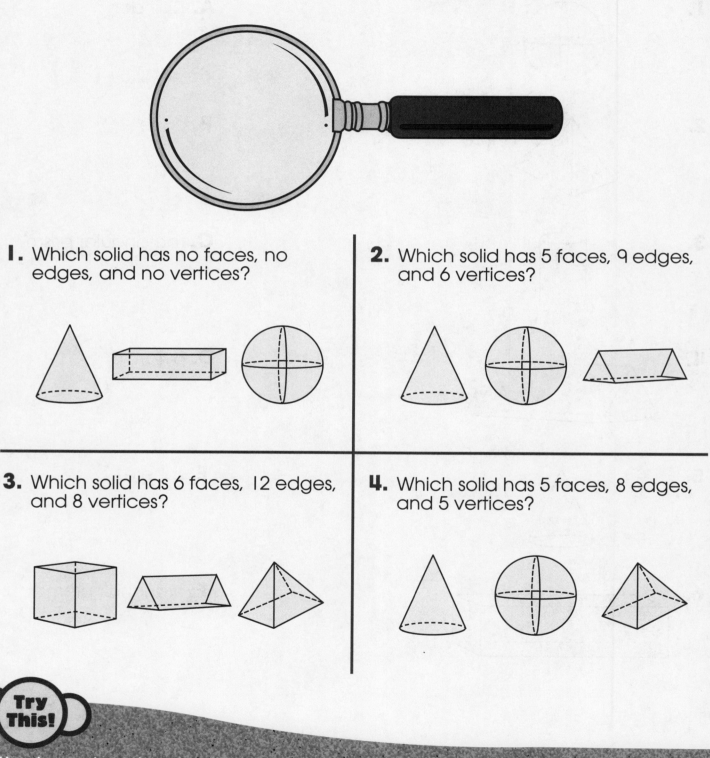

1. Which solid has no faces, no edges, and no vertices?

2. Which solid has 5 faces, 9 edges, and 6 vertices?

3. Which solid has 6 faces, 12 edges, and 8 vertices?

4. Which solid has 5 faces, 8 edges, and 5 vertices?

Try This!

How is a rectangular prism like a cube? How are they different? Write your answer on another sheet of paper.

Is Your Foot a Foot?

Directions: Circle **inches** or **feet**.

1. 8 **inches** or 8 **feet**

2. 4 **inches** or 4 **feet**

3. 9 **inches** or 9 **feet**

4. 10 **inches** or 10 **feet**

5. 20 **inches** or 20 **feet**

6. 12 **inches** or 12 **feet**

Try This!

Find objects that are about 1 foot, 2 feet, 3 feet, and 4 feet in length.
Draw a picture of each object on another sheet of paper. Label each picture.

Pool Party

Directions: Solve each problem.

1. David's pool is 40 feet long. He can swim 26 feet without stopping. How many more feet does he need to swim?

2. David's pool is 50 feet from the deck. If he walks 30 feet and wants to tiptoe the rest of the way, how many feet will he tiptoe?

3. David's family bought a volleyball net for the pool. It came in three 18-inch sections that snap together. How long is the net?

4. The diving board is 5 feet long. How many inches long is it?

On another sheet of paper, draw a picture of one of the problems above.

For Good Measure

Directions: Circle the correct amounts.

1 pint = 2 cups	1 quart = 2 pints

1.

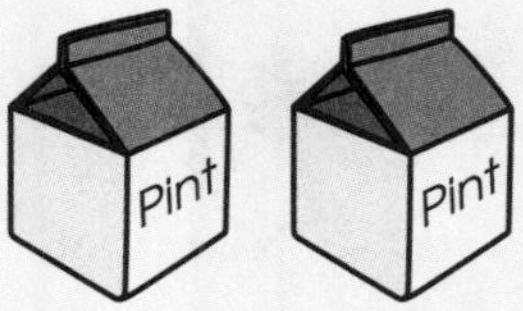

Pint Pint =

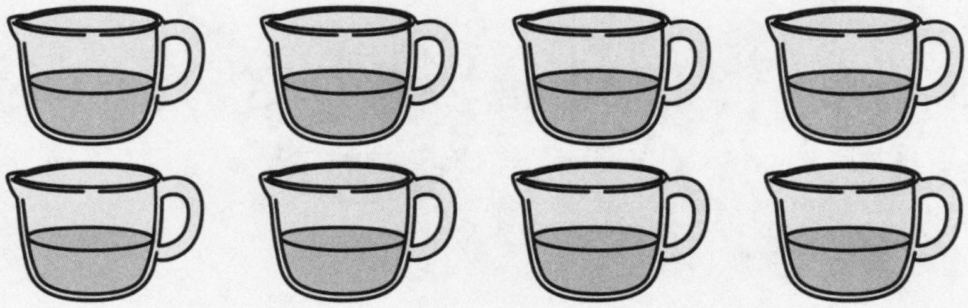

2.

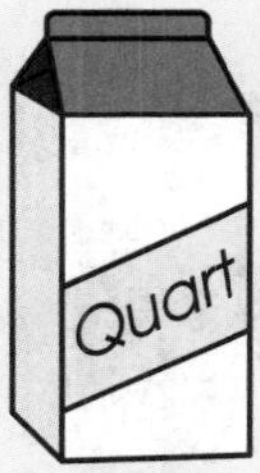

Quart =

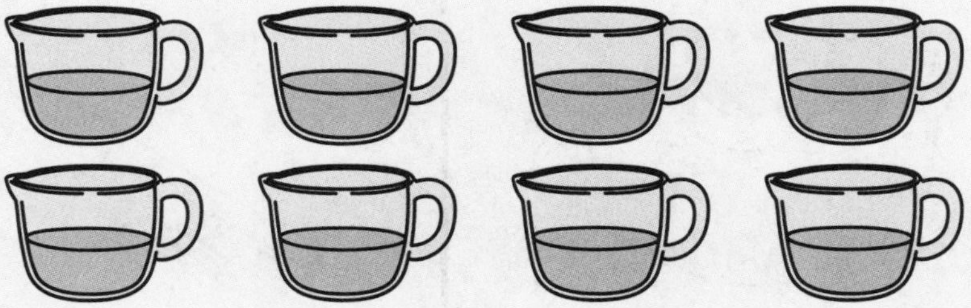

3.

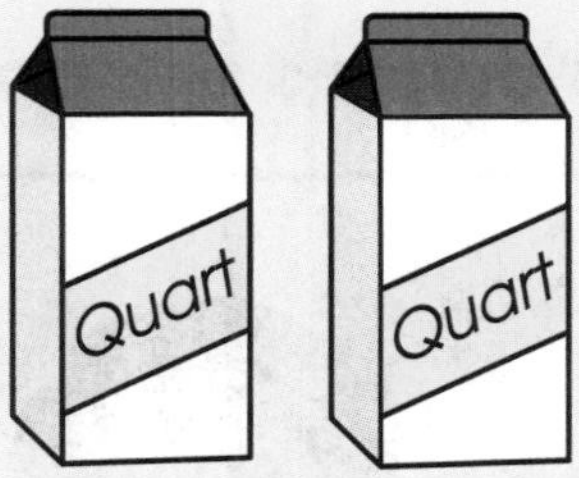

Quart Quart =

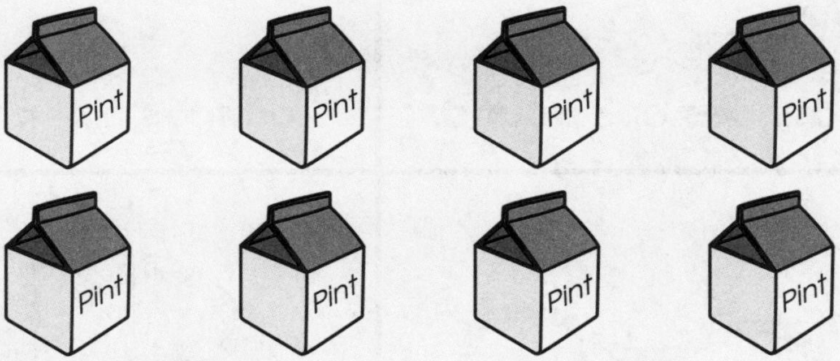

4.

Quart Quart Quart =

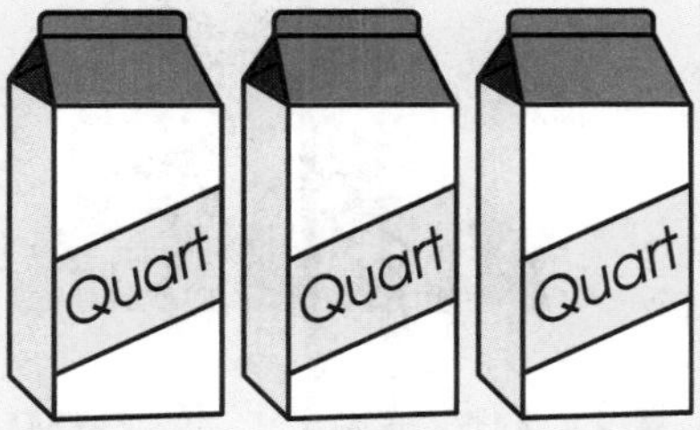

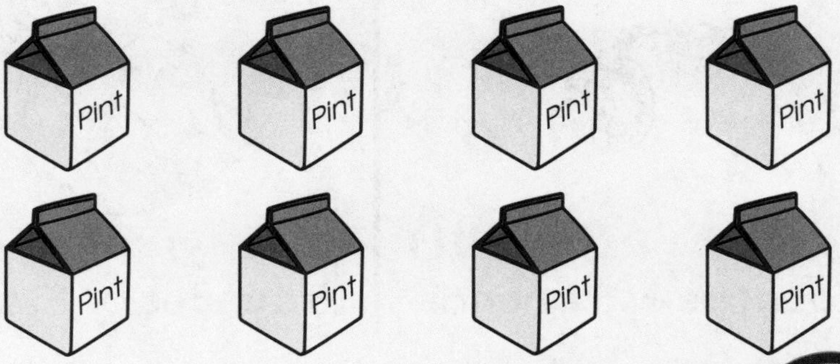

Try This!

On another sheet of paper, draw pictures of things you measure in cups, pints, and quarts.

Just "Weight"!

Directions: Circle **ounces** or **pounds**.

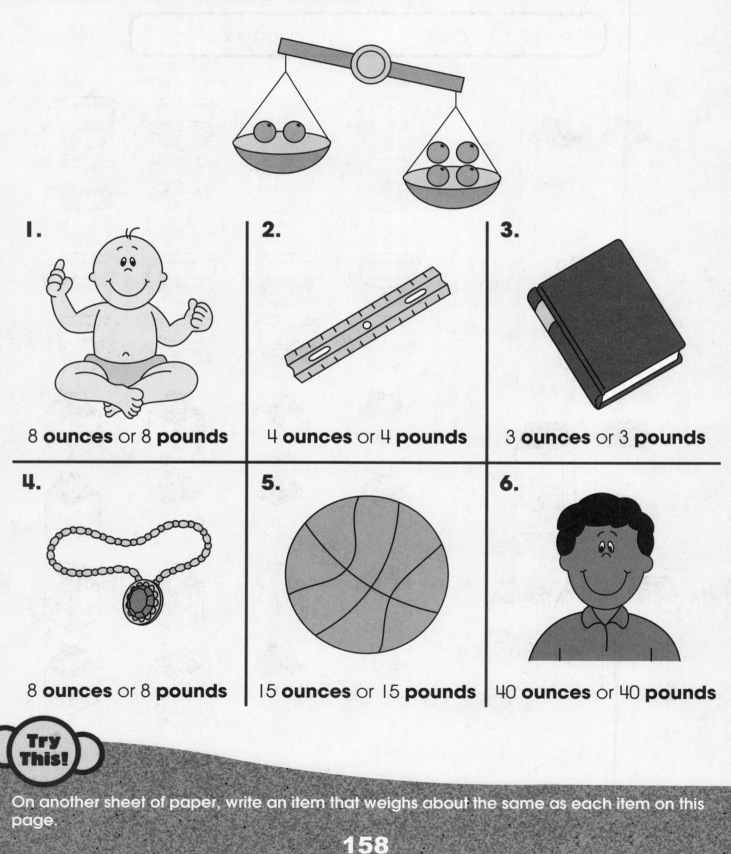

1.
8 **ounces** or 8 **pounds**

2.
4 **ounces** or 4 **pounds**

3.
3 **ounces** or 3 **pounds**

4.
8 **ounces** or 8 **pounds**

5.
15 **ounces** or 15 **pounds**

6.
40 **ounces** or 40 **pounds**

Try This!

On another sheet of paper, write an item that weighs about the same as each item on this page.

Weighty Problems

Directions: Solve each problem.

1. Adrian needs 2 pounds of apples to make applesauce. Sixteen ounces are in a pound. She put the apples on the scale and saw they weighed 20 ounces. How many more ounces of apples does she need?

2. Adrian needs a pound of vegetables for a salad. She has carrots that weigh 6 ounces and celery that weighs 7 ounces. How many more ounces of vegetables does she need?

3. Adrian bought a 5-pound bag of potatoes. If each potato weighs about 4 ounces, about how many potatoes were in the bag?

4. When Adrian left the store, she had 30 pounds of food in 5 bags. If the bags each weighed the same amount, how much did each bag weigh?

On another sheet of paper, make a list of five things you weigh in ounces and five things you weigh in pounds.

Time for Fun

Directions: Write the letter of each clock on the line above its time to see what happens when you have fun.

1. **I**

2. **E**

3. **T**

4. **F**

5. **S**

6. **E**

7. **M**

8. **I**

9. **L**

| 10:00 | 3:30 | 5:30 | 6:00 | 12:30 | 9:30 | 7:00 | 2:30 | 3:00 |

Try This!

On another sheet of paper, write what you do at 6:30 in the morning and what you do at 6:30 at night.

Late-Night Snacks

Directions: Discover what these night animals eat by drawing a line from each animal to the food that matches its feeding time.

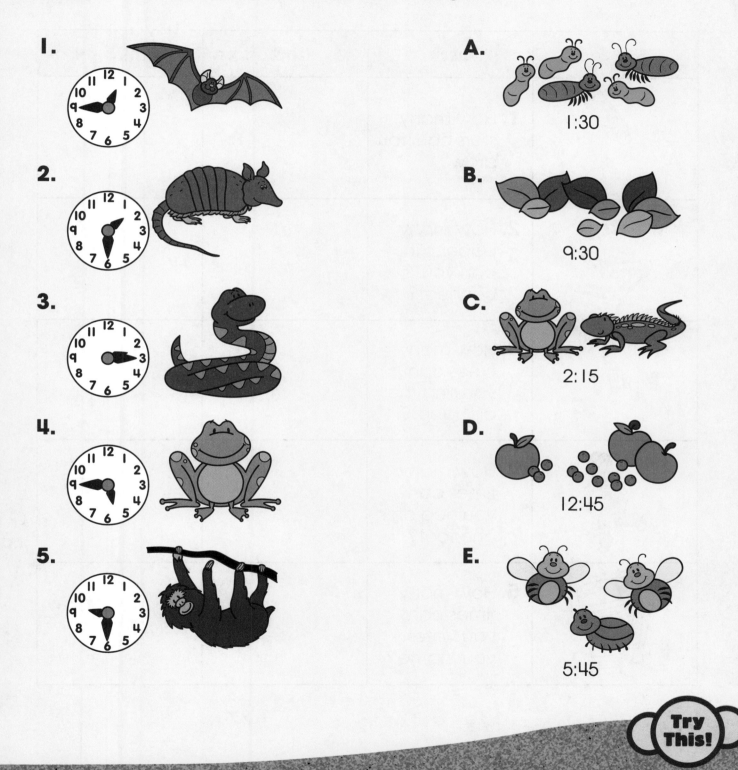

1.

2.

3.

4.

5.

A.

1:30

B.

9:30

C.

2:15

D.

12:45

E.

5:45

Try This!

On another sheet of paper, write the times you eat and the foods you eat at each time.

In a Minute

Directions: Predict how many times you can do each activity in one minute. Then, try it out.

	Task	My Prediction	Actual Number
	**1.** How many stars can you draw?		
	2. How many paper clips can you connect?		
	3. How many times can you sing the alphabet?		
	4. How many times can you hop on one foot?		
	5. How many times can you write your name?		

Try This!

On another sheet of paper, make a list of 10 things you can do in a minute.

Time for Fairy Tales

Directions: Read each word problem. Draw hands on the clocks to show the starting and ending times.

1.

The itsy-bitsy spider climbed up the waterspout.
He started to climb at 3:00. It took him 30 minutes.

Starting Time   Ending Time

2.

Little Bo Peep lost her sheep. She started looking for them at 10:00 in the morning. It took her four hours to find them.

Starting Time   Ending Time

3.

Little Boy Blue fell asleep under the haystack. He fell asleep at 2:15. He slept for 2 hours and 15 minutes.

Starting Time   Ending Time

4.

Little Miss Muffet sat on her tuffet, eating her curds and whey. She started eating at 7:00. It took her 45 minutes to eat.

Starting Time   Ending Time

Try This!

On another sheet of paper, create three more time problems using your favorite characters. Ask a friend to solve the problems.

What Are the Chances?

Directions: Read each sentence. Circle **likely** or **unlikely**.

1. A cat will purr when it is happy.   **likely**   **unlikely**

2. A hamster will grow as large as a dog.   **likely**   **unlikely**

3. A goldfish will walk on its hands.   **likely**   **unlikely**

4. A snake will grow fur.   **likely**   **unlikely**

5. A parrot will sit on its perch.   **likely**   **unlikely**

6. A horse will eat hay.   **likely**   **unlikely**

7. A dog will wag its tail.   **likely**   **unlikely**

8. An elephant will fly.   **likely**   **unlikely**

Write one more likely sentence and one more unlikely sentence on another sheet of paper.

Which Chip?

Directions: Look at the chips in each bag. Write the color of the chip you are most likely to pull from the bag.

1. _____

2. _____

3. _____

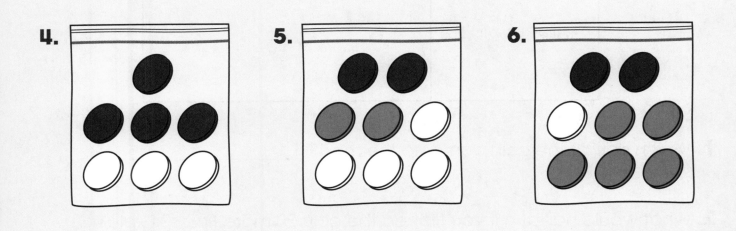

4. _____

5. _____

6. _____

Try This!

On another sheet of paper, write a fraction to show how many blue chips are in each bag.

Let's Flip!

Directions: Flip 1 coin 20 times. Record the results using tally marks.

heads	
tails	

1. Which side of the coin came up the most? _____

2. What would happen if you flipped the coin 20 more times? Explain.

_____

_____

Try This!

Flip two coins 20 times. Record the results. Which combination of coins came up more often? What do you think would happen if you flipped the coins 20 more times?

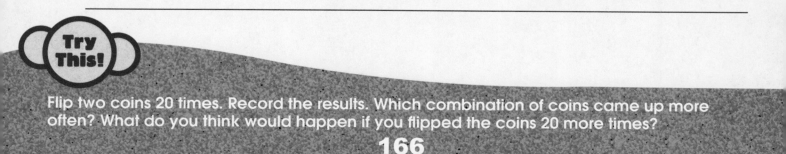

Playground Fun

Directions: Look at the map of a playground. Then, follow the directions.

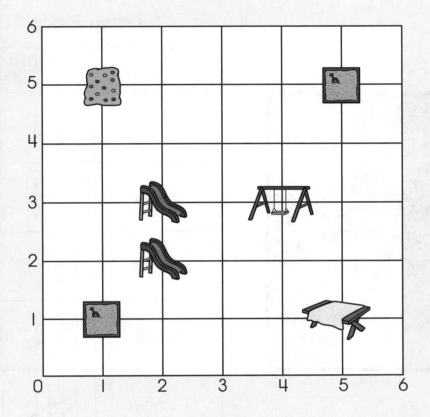

1. Draw a shovel beside the sandbox at (5, 5).

2. Draw another slide at (1, 3).

3. Draw three trash cans at (5, 2).

4. Write the coordinates for the rock climbing wall. _____

5. Write the coordinates of the swings. _____

Try This!

On a sheet of grid paper, make a map of your school playground.
Label five of the places on your map using coordinates.

Doing Our Part

Directions: Read the chart. Then, answer the questions.

Trash Bags Filled

Name	Number of Trash Bags
Zack	~~||||~~ |
Wren	~~||||~~
Tripp	|||
Stone	~~||||~~ ||
Renee	~~||||~~

1. What information is shown on the chart? _____

2. Who collected the most trash bags? _____

3. Who collected the fewest trash bags? _____

4. Who collected the same amount of trash bags? _____

5. How many trash bags were collected altogether? _____

On another sheet of paper, make a list of at least five more ways you can do your part to help Earth.

Ice-Cream Sales

Directions: Read the bar graph. Then, write two true sentences about the information on the graph.

Strawberry

Mint

Chocolate

Vanilla

Ice-Cream Sales for July 10

1. _____

_____

2. _____

_____

Try This!

If each cone cost $1.00, how much money did the store make?
Show your work on another sheet of paper.

Earth Day

Directions: Read the graph. Then, answer the questions.

Neighborhood Recycling—Week 1

Glass Bottles	♳ ♳ ♳
Aluminum Cans	♳ ♳ ♳ ♳ ♳
Newspapers	♳ ♳ ♳ ♳ ♳ ♳ ♳ ♳
Plastic Containers	♳ ♳

♳ = 10

1. What does the ♳ mean if you see it on a container? _____

2. How many glass bottles were recycled? _____

3. How many more cans were recycled than bottles? _____

4. How many items were recycled altogether? _____

If the neighborhood collected the same amount for two weeks, how many items would have been recycled altogether?

School Is Cool!

Directions: Read the pie graph. Then, answer the questions.

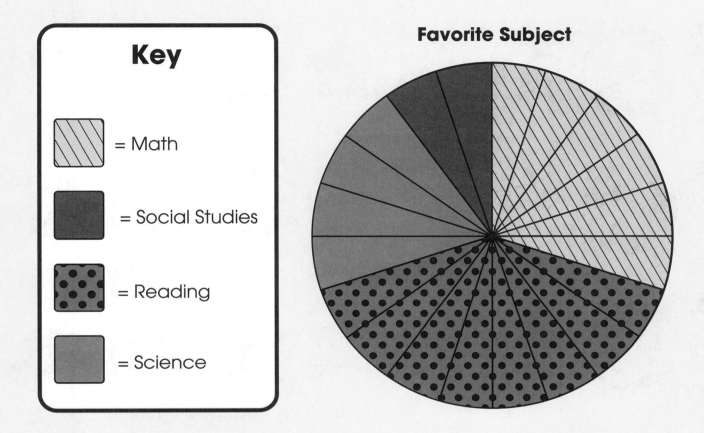

Key

= Math

= Social Studies

= Reading

= Science

Favorite Subject

1. What subject do the most students like best? _____

2. How many students voted for math as their favorite subject? _____

3. How many students voted for science and math? _____

4. How many more students voted for reading than social studies? _____

5. How many students voted altogether? _____

Try This!

On another sheet of paper, write two more sentences about the information on this graph.

Star Patterns

Directions: Read the rules. Write the missing numbers.

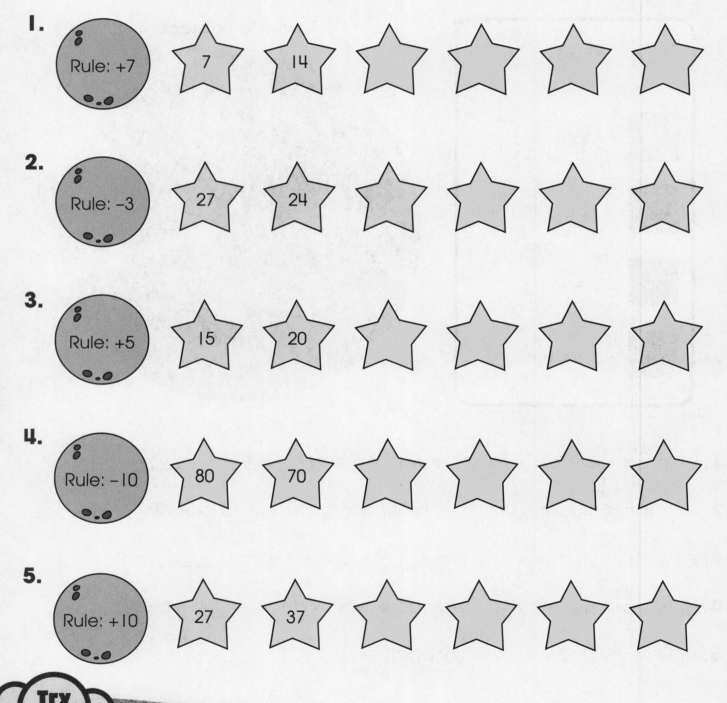

1. Rule: +7 — 7, 14, ☆, ☆, ☆, ☆

2. Rule: −3 — 27, 24, ☆, ☆, ☆, ☆

3. Rule: +5 — 15, 20, ☆, ☆, ☆, ☆

4. Rule: −10 — 80, 70, ☆, ☆, ☆, ☆

5. Rule: +10 — 27, 37, ☆, ☆, ☆, ☆

Try This!

Use a calculator to add each row of stars.
Write the totals for each row.

Munching Machine

Directions: Write the missing numbers.

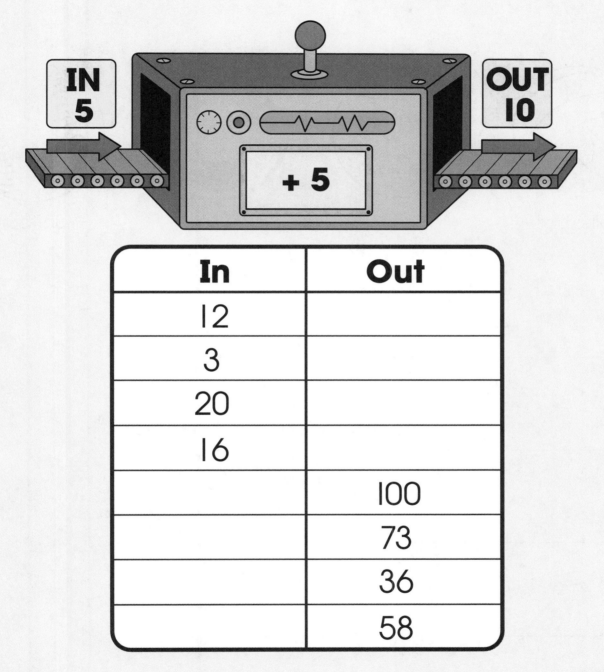

In	Out
12	
3	
20	
16	
	100
	73
	36
	58

Try This!

On another sheet of paper, design another machine with another pattern.
Write five numbers that go into and come out of your machine.

Having a Ball

Directions: Sarah must decide which sports she will play in summer camp. Although four are offered, she can choose only three. Write the different combinations of sports that Sarah can play during camp.

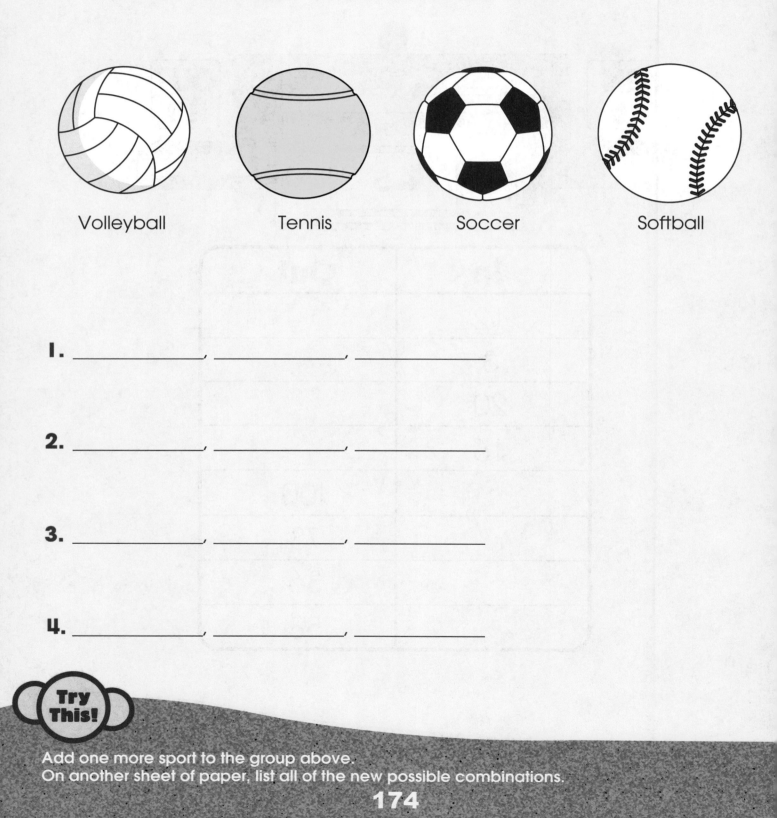

Volleyball   Tennis   Soccer   Softball

1. _____, _____, _____

2. _____, _____, _____

3. _____, _____, _____

4. _____, _____, _____

Try This!

Add one more sport to the group above.
On another sheet of paper, list all of the new possible combinations.

Under the Stars

Directions: Jimmy, Matthew, and Miguel are camping. Use the clues to figure out who is in each sleeping bag. Write their names on the sleeping bags.

1. Matthew is not next to Jimmy.

2. Jimmy wanted to sleep next to the fire.

3. Miguel chose the middle sleeping bag.

Try This!

Make a list of all of the things you would like to do if you went camping with friends.
Use another sheet of paper.

Portraits of Presidents

Directions: Write the name of each president under the correct picture frame. Then, draw a portrait of each president.

1. George Washington's portrait is above Franklin Roosevelt's portrait.

2. Franklin Roosevelt's portrait is on the left side.

3. Barack Obama's portrait is under the president whose image is on the penny.

4. John Adams's portrait is in the middle of the top row.

5. Abraham Lincoln's portrait is to the right of John Adams's portrait.

6. George W. Bush's portrait is under Adams's portrait.

Try This!

On another sheet of paper, write another clue to tell where Abraham Lincoln's portrait would go.

Answer Key

Page 10

1. whistle, whiskers, whisk; 2. shoe, shelf, shell; 3. chin, cheese, chimney; 4. thumb, thermometer, three.

Page 11

1. strong; 2. shrub; 3. throne; 4. shrunk; 5. thread; 6. strap.

Page 12

1. sock; 2. match; 3. duck; 4. patch; 5. crack.

Page 13

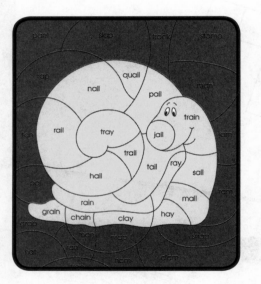

Page 14

Short e words: hen, yes, mess, pet; Long e words: three, beach, peach, tree.

Page 15

Green: trick, spill, lip, kick; yellow: ride, bike, lion, kite, lime.

Page 16

1. frog; 2. rope; 3. fox; 4. stove; 5. rod; 6. rose.

Page 17

1. ~~duck~~; 2. ~~tub~~; 3. ~~truck~~; 4. ~~cluck~~; 5. ~~doughnut~~; 6. ~~club~~; 7. ~~cut~~; 8. ~~luck~~.

Page 18

ou words: loud, sound, shout, bounce; ow words: crowd, growl, down, brown.

Page 19

took words: look, wood, book, hook; moon words: school, room, zoo, goose.

Page 20

1. coin; 2. soil; 3. boy; 4. choice; 5. toy; 6. joy.

Page 21

1. 2; 2. 2; 3. 2; 4. 1; 5. 2; 6. 1; 7. 1; 8. 2; 9. 1; 10. 2; 11. 1; 12. 2.

Page 22

1. bi; 2. pre; 3. re; 4. un.

Page 23
1. joyful; 2. colorless; 3. hopeful; 4. graceful; 5. careless; 6. sleepless; 7. delightful; 8. powerful.

Page 24
1. bak<u>er</u>; 2. doct<u>or</u>; 3. auth<u>or</u>; 4. catch<u>er</u>; 5. photograph<u>er</u>; 6. illustrat<u>or</u>.

Page 25
Person: mother, doctor, teacher, baby; Place: cave, school, Washington, playground; Thing: car, desk, statue, ball.

Page 26
Answers will vary.

Page 27
1. chickens; 2. horses; 3. fences; 4. shovels; 5. ducks; 6. eggs; 7. cows; 8. haystacks.

Page 28
1. foxes; 2. bushes; 3. buses; 4. lunches; 5. sandwiches; 6. boxes; Sentences will vary.

Page 29

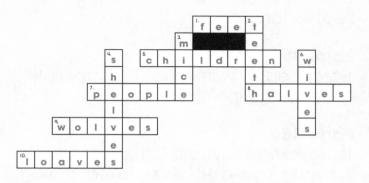

Page 30
1. She; 2. He; 3. It; 4. We; 5. They; 6. It.

Page 31
1. gathered; 2. built; 3. blazed; 4. peeled; 5. handed; 6. roasted.

Page 32
1. is: green; 2. sing: blue; 3. am: green; 4. are: green; 5. chirps: blue; 6. chomps: blue.

Page 33
1. swing; 2. jumps; 3. play; 4. slide; 5. hoots; 6. hops; 7. gallops; 8. scamper.

Page 34

1. swept; 2. drew; 3. made; 4. went; 5. slept; 6. ran; 7. swam; 8. came.

Page 35

1. stopped; 2. swimming; 3. clapped; 4. hopped; 5. skipping; 6. running.

Page 36

1. recycling, recycled; 2. taping, taped; 3. saving, saved; 4. biking, biked; 5. filing, filed; 6. smiling, smiled; 7. baking, baked; 8. skating, skated.

Page 37

1. are; 2. are; 3. am; 4. is; 5. is; 6. am.

Page 38

1. were; 2. was; 3. were; 4. were; 5. was; 6. were; 7. were; 8. was.

Page 39

Answers will vary.

Page 40

1. cold; 2. colder; 3. coldest; 4. big; 5. bigger; 6. biggest.

Page 41

a: pear, kiwifruit, banana, lemon; an: apple, orange, apricot, avocado.

Page 42

1. Breakfast is at 7:30 each morning. 2. You must clean your cabin. 3. Every camper needs a buddy. 4. Three campers can ride in a canoe. 5. All lights will be out at 9:00.

Page 43

1. I like to hike. 2. Today is my birthday. 3. Sarah likes to solve mysteries. 4. The bee stung my finger. 5. My mother is a nurse.

Page 44

1. How old are you? 2. Are you in second grade? 3. Who is your teacher? 4. What is your favorite book? 5. Where do you live?

Page 45

1. I am so excited! 2. Our team won the game! 3. My brother is on the team, too. 4. My friend watched the game. 5. We received a huge trophy! 6. Then, we went for pizza. 7. I ate a piece of pizza. 8. Today was the best day ever!

Page 46

1. Davis, Destini, and Dylan went on a picnic. 2. They brought a basket, a blanket, and a radio. 3. They ate sandwiches, pickles, and fruit. 4. They saw Emory, Juan, and Brian hiking. 5. They flew kites, walked, and gathered flowers together. 6. They want to plan another picnic for Sunday, Monday, or Wednesday.

Page 47

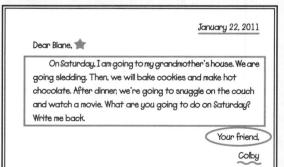

January 22, 2011

Dear Blane,

On Saturday, I am going to my grandmother's house. We are going sledding. Then, we will bake cookies and make hot chocolate. After dinner, we're going to snuggle on the couch and watch a movie. What are you going to do on Saturday? Write me back.

Your friend,

Colby

Page 48
1. "The train is here!" exclaimed Justin.
2. "Can we get on the train?" asked
Cara. 3. "Not yet," warned Mrs. Rossi. 4.
"All aboard!" shouted the conductor.
5. "Now we can get on the train," said
Mrs. Rossi. 6. "Tickets, please," said the
conductor. 7. "Here are our tickets," said
Mrs. Rossi. 8. "I love riding the train," said
Justin. 9. "Me too!" agreed Cara. 10.
"Can we ride it again tomorrow?" asked
Justin.

Page 49
1. We're, a; 2. can't, no; 3. I'm, a; 4.
Don't, o; 5. isn't, o; 6. She's, i; 7. You'll, wi;
8. It's, i.

Page 50

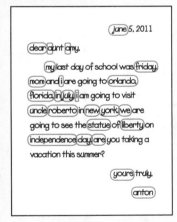

Page 51
1. sad; 2. pretty; 3. sleepy; 4. silly; 5. small;
6. frightening.

Page 52
1. My teacher lost a box of magnets. 2.
Those two objects moved apart. 3. Cory
emptied the bucket. 4. We used cold
water for the experiment. 5. That boat
sinks.

Page 53
1. You're; 2. your; 3. You're; 4. your; 5.
You're; 6. your; 7. your; 8. you're.

Page 54
1. there; 2. They're; 3. Their; 4. They're; 5.
They're; 6. Their; 7. Their; 8. there.

Page 55
1. to; 2. two; 3. to; 4. two; 5. too; 6. too.

Page 56
1. sandbox; 2. hallway; 3. notebook; 4.
raincoat; 5. bedroom.

Page 57
1. apple; 2. boy; 3. cup; 4. goat; 5. hat;
6. lion; 7. ship; 8. truck.

Page 58
Facts (orange): Pumpkins have seeds.
Pumpkins grow on vines. A pumpkin is
a fruit. Opinions (yellow): Pumpkin pie
is best. Pumpkin seeds are tasty. Big
pumpkins are better.

Page 59
Answers will vary.

Page 60
Answers will vary.

Page 61
1. nonfiction; 2. to inform.

Page 62
1. fiction; 2. to entertain; 3. Flying Fish.

Page 63
Exaggerations (underlined): An apple tree would grow by morning. The apples would peel themselves and jump into the nearest pie shell. Sweaters would spring up overnight. It grew so big that Grace opened a café inside of it.

Page 64
"Why Dogs' Ears Hang Down."

Page 65
Answers will vary.

Page 66
Order of pictures: 3, 1, 2, 4; 1. to the store; 2. to buy an apple; 3. 25¢.

Page 67
1. The flashlight fish uncovers its lights. 2. The flashlight fish swims in a straight line. 3. The flashlight fish covers its lights. 4. The flashlight fish turns and races away.

Page 68
1. All insects have six legs. 2. Different insects eat different things. 3. Insects live in different kinds of homes.

Page 69
Astronauts Neil Armstrong and Buzz Aldrin were the first men to walk on the moon.

Page 70

One crisp morning in October, we drove to the mountains to pick apples. We took Daddy's old pickup truck. When we got to the orchard, we spied hundreds of trees filled with apples! Some were golden yellow and some were bright red. We even saw some that were green. I took a bite from one of the apples. It tasted so sweet. The juice dribbled down my chin. We picked three bushels of apples. Then, we went home to bake some pies.

Page 71
1. France; 2. July 4, 1776; 3. New York Harbor; 4. freedom.

Page 72
1. The wind blew. 2. Rosa filled the balloons with helium. 3. It was my birthday. 4. The clown made silly balloon animals. 5. The child let go of the string. 6. The balloon popped.

Page 73
1. People; 2. Animals; 3. Wind; 4. Water.

Page 74
1. A; 2. B.

Page 75
Answers will vary.

Page 76
1. B; 2. A; 3. C.

Page 77
1. B; 2. A; 3. E; 4. C; 5. D; 6. F.

Page 78
1. a bear; 2. The little dark eyes were part of a great big furry face. He saw that the eyes were part of something tall when it stood on its two legs. "Grrr ..." growled the eyes.

Page 79
1. C; 2. D; 3. A; 4. B.

Page 80
The story is about a gorilla that learns to communicate with sign language.

Page 81
The story is about a boy who finds a spider.

Page 82
Answers will vary.

Page 83

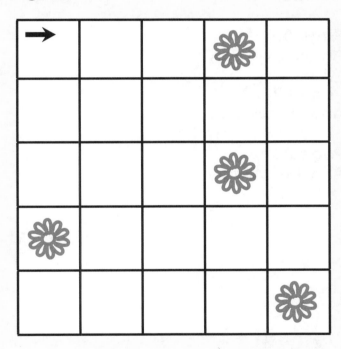

Page 84

Page 85
1. to inform; 2. to inform; 3. to entertain;
4. to persuade.

Page 86
Answers will vary.

Page 87
Answers will vary.

Page 88
Answers will vary.

Page 89
It is a time to be thankful. Many families gather for dinner. ~~Many trees lose leaves in the autumn.~~ Some families eat turkey for Thanksgiving dinner. ~~November is the eleventh month.~~ Some people enjoy pumpkin pie. ~~Valentine's Day is celebrated in February.~~

Page 90
Answers will vary.

Page 91
<u>Spelling</u> can be hard. It is not <u>easy</u> to think about spelling each <u>word</u> right when you are <u>busy</u> thinking about what to write. That is why it is good to edit <u>your</u> <u>writing</u>. It is like having a second <u>chance</u> to do it <u>right</u>.

Page 92
Answers will vary.

Page 93
Answers will vary. Possible answers include: snow; sky; hand; sight.

Page 94
Answers will vary.

Page 95
Answers will vary.

Page 96
Answers will vary.

Page 98
1. 1 ten, 2 ones; 2. 1 ten, 3 ones; 3. 2 tens, 2 ones; 4. 1 ten, 5 ones; 5. 4 tens, 3 ones; 6. 3 tens, 1 one.

Page 99
1. 663; 2. 421; 3. 521; 4. 653; 5. 641; 6. 532; 7. 543; 8. 211; 9. 621.

Page 100
1. 2: 2,000; 2. 4: 4,000; 3. 3: 3,000; 4. 4: 4,000; 5. 1: 1,000; 6. 5: 5,000; 7. 6: 6,000; 8. 3: 3,000; 9. 7: 7,000.

Page 101

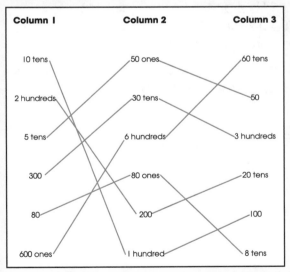

Page 102
1. C; 2. E; 3. B; 4. A; 5. D.

Page 103
Row 1: 59, 26, 19, 90; Row 2: 19, 11, 90; Row 3: 50, 66, 100, 62; Colored balloons: 26, 90, 90, 50, 66, 100, 62; an **X** on the rest.

Page 104

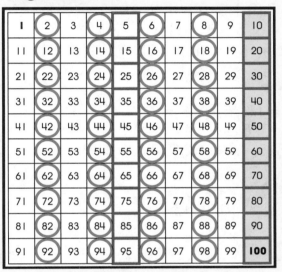

Page 105
1. 6, 12; 2. 16, 22; 3. 80, 84, 86; 4. 20, 30; 5. 50, 60, 70; 6. 60, 70, 80.

Page 106
1. 52; 2. 20; 3. 76; 4. 29; 5. 98; 6. 53; 7. 274;
8. 888; 9. 194; 10. 370; 11. 7,001; 12. 1,302;
13. 334; 14. 3,100.

Page 107
1. 601, 610, 623, 632; 2. 898, 899, 909, 990;
3. 91, 111, 121, 131; 4. 305, 350, 503, 530.

Page 108
red: 5 + 7, 9 + 3, 8 + 4, 4 + 8, 6 + 6; blue:
9 + 4, 7 + 6, 5 + 8; yellow: 7 + 7, 8 + 6;
green: 6 + 9, 9 + 6, 7 + 8.

Page 109
1. 5 + 6 = 11; 2. 7 + 4 = 11; 3. 6 + 3 = 9; 4. 9
+ 4 = 13; 5. 5 + 7 = 12; 6. 9 + 5 = 14; 7. 4 +
6 = 10; 8. 5 + 8 = 13; 9. 7 + 6 = 13.

Page 110
1. 12; 2. 8; 3. 10; 4. 13.

Page 111
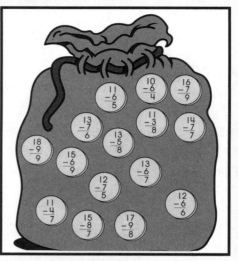

Page 112
1. 10 – 4 = 6 kittens left; 2. 12 – 3 = 9
rabbits left; 3. 11 – 7 = 4 birds left; 4. 14 –
9 = 5 birds left.

Page 113
1. 2 + 7 = 9, 7 + 2 = 9, 9 – 7 = 2, 9 – 2 = 7;
2. 8 + 9 = 17, 9 + 8 = 17, 17 – 8 = 9, 17 – 9
= 8; 3. 9 + 5 = 14, 5 + 9 = 14, 14 – 9 = 5, 14
– 5 = 9; 4. 8 + 6 = 14, 6 + 8 = 14, 14 – 6 = 8,
14 – 8 = 6; 5. 7 + 6 = 13, 6 + 7 = 13, 13 – 7
= 6, 13 – 6 = 7.

Answer Key

Page 114

1. 7; 2. 8; 3. 8; 4. 8.

Page 115

1. 12; 2. 13; 3. 19; 4. 16; 5. 11; 6. 12; 7. 17; 8. 17; 9. 19; 10. 14.

Page 116

1. subtract; 6 – 4 = 2; 2 swings are empty; 2. subtract; 8 – 3 = 5; 5 more steps; 3. add; 5 + 5 = 10; 10 times; 4. add; 3 + 3 = 6; 6 children are on benches.

Page 117

1st Place = 30 feet; 2nd Place= 27 feet; 3rd Place = 24 feet.

Page 118

1. 12 tens: 40 + 80 = 120; 2. 7 tens: 10 + 60 = 70; 3. 5 tens: 30 + 20 =50; 4. 11 tens: 70 + 40 = 110; 5. 7 tens: 60 + 10 = 70.

Page 119

1. 39; 2. 85; 3. 99; 4. 76; 5. 88; 6. 78.

Page 120

Page 121

1. 26; 2. 26; 3. 21; 4. 25; 5. 65; 6. 12.

Page 122

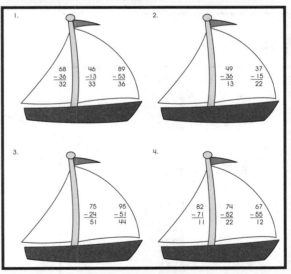

Page 123

1. 17 + 26 = 43, 43 horses and hens; 2. 19 + 15 = 34, 34 sheep; 3. 25 + 17 = 42, 42 cows and horses; 4. 25 + 17 + 19 + 26 = 87, 87 animals.

Page 124

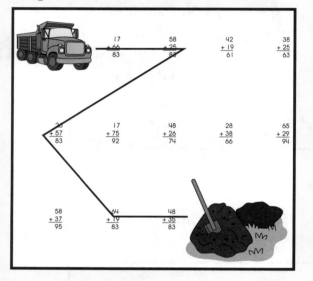

Page 125

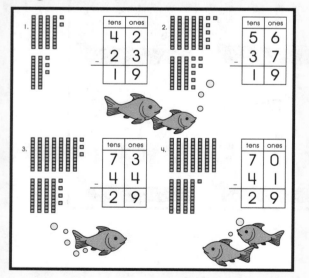

Page 126

top to bottom and left to right: 12, 63, 43, 56, 22, 33, 17, 69, 54, 27, 37, 24.

Page 127

quarter: quarter, 25¢, $0.25, twenty-five cents; dime: 10¢, ten cents, $0.10, dime; nickel: 5¢, nickel, five cents, $0.05; penny: one cent, penny, 1¢, $0.01.

Page 128

1. D; 2. F; 3. B; 4. G; 5. H; 6. A; 7. E; 8. C.

Page 129

1. 40¢, 1 quarter, 1 dime, 1 nickel; 2. 35¢, 1 quarter, 1 dime; 3. 60¢, 2 quarters, 1 dime; 4. 72¢, 2 quarters, 2 dimes, 2 pennies.

Page 130

1. 1 half-dollar, 2 quarters, 2 dimes, 1 nickel; 2. 3 quarters, 1 dime, 2 nickels, 4 pennies; 3. 4 half-dollars, 3 quarters, 4 dimes, 2 nickels; 4. 1 half-dollar, 3 quarters, 5 dimes, 2 nickels; 5. 4 quarters, 1 dime, 1 nickel, 3 pennies.

Page 131

1. $1.35; 2. $1.15; 3. $2.30; 4. $2.50.

Page 132

1. 4 quarters; 2. 4 dimes, 1 nickel; 3. 3 quarters, 3 nickels; 4. 1 quarter, 2 nickels, 1 penny.

Page 133

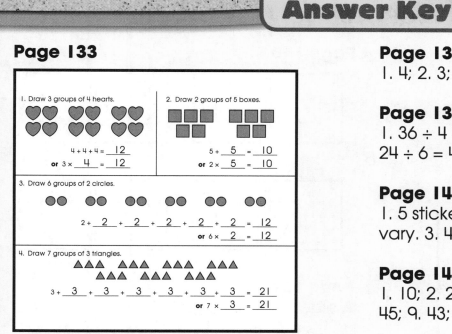

Page 134

1. C; 2. B; 3. A; 4. D; 5. E; 6. F.

Page 135

yellow: 4 x 5, 5 x 4, 20 x 1, 10 x 2; green: 6 x 5, 5 x 6, 10 x 3, 30 x 1; purple: 6 x 2, 2 x 6, 3 x 4, 4 x 3; red: 2 x 3, 3 x 2, 6 x 1; blue: 2 x 8, 8 x 2, 4 x 4, 16 x 1; orange: 6 x 4, 4 x 6, 8 x 3, 3 x 8.

Page 136

1. 36 stripes; 2. 72 spots; 3. 21 stripes; 4. 49 spots; 5. 72 stripes; 6. 4 zebras.

Page 137

1. 5; 2. 4; 3. 4; 4. 5.

Page 138

1. 4; 2. 3; 3. 9.

Page 139

1. 36 ÷ 4 = 9; 2. 5 x 8 = 40; 3. 6 x 5 = 30; 4. 24 ÷ 6 = 4.

Page 140

1. 5 stickers in each row; 2. Answers will vary. 3. 42 stickers; 4. 167 stickers.

Page 141

1. 10; 2. 26; 3. 35; 4. 6; 5. 45; 6. 95; 7. 45; 8. 45; 9. 43; 10. 4.

Page 142

1. $\frac{1}{8}$; 2. $\frac{1}{2}$; 3. $\frac{1}{16}$; 4. $\frac{1}{4}$.

Page 143

Row 1: $\frac{1}{2}$, $\frac{1}{2}$, $\frac{1}{4}$; Row 2: $\frac{1}{3}$, $\frac{1}{3}$, $\frac{1}{2}$; Row 3: $\frac{1}{2}$, $\frac{1}{3}$, $\frac{1}{4}$.

Page 144

1. $\frac{1}{4}$ pink, $\frac{3}{4}$ orange; 2. $\frac{3}{5}$ blue, $\frac{2}{5}$ red.

Page 145

1. 12 pictures of his family; 2. 45 pictures are of boys; 3. 7 pictures of her brother; 4. 7 pictures on each page.

Page 146

10 circles; 8 rectangles; 2 triangles; 19 squares; 4 rhombuses; 2 ovals.

Page 147

Answers will vary.

Page 148

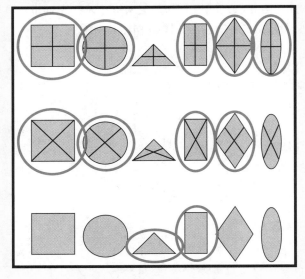

Page 149

1. congruent; 2. congruent; 3. noncongruent; 4. noncongruent; 5. noncongruent; 6. congruent.

Page 150

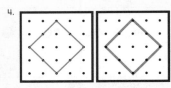

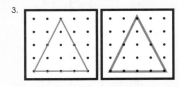

Page 151

1. slide; 2. turn; 3. flip; 4. flip.

Page 152

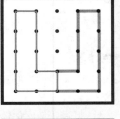

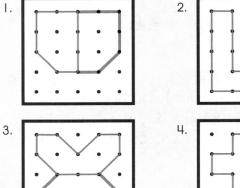

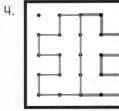

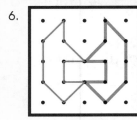

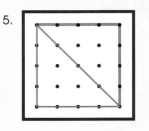

Answer Key

Page 153
1. E; 2. D; 3. A; 4. F; 5. B; 6. C.

Page 154
1. sphere; 2. triangular prism; 3. cube; 4. rectangular pyramid.

Page 155
1. 8 inches; 2. 4 feet; 3. 9 inches; 4. 10 feet; 5. 20 feet; 6. 12 inches.

Page 156
1. 14 feet; 2. 20 feet; 3. 54 inches; 4. 60 inches.

Page 157
1. 2 pints = 4 cups; 2. 1 quart = 8 cups; 3. 2 quarts = 4 pints; 4. 3 quarts = 6 pints.

Page 158
1. 8 pounds; 2. 4 ounces; 3. 3 pounds; 4. 8 ounces; 5. 15 ounces; 6. 40 pounds.

Page 159
1. 12 ounces; 2. 3 ounces; 3. 20 potatoes; 4. 6 pounds.

Page 160
Time flies.

Page 161
1. D; 2. A; 3. C; 4. E; 5. B.

Page 162
Answers will vary.

Page 163

1.

Starting Time   Ending Time

2.

Starting Time   Ending Time

3.

Starting Time   Ending Time

4.

Starting Time   Ending Time

Page 164
1. likely; 2. unlikely; 3. unlikely; 4. unlikely; 5. likely; 6. likely; 7. likely; 8. unlikely.

Page 165
1. blue; 2. white; 3. same chance of blue and white; 4. blue; 5. white; 6. red.

Answer Key

Page 166
Answers will vary.

Page 167

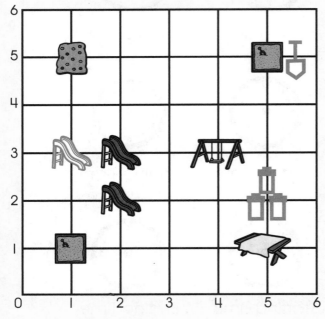

4. (1, 5); 5. (4, 3).

Page 168
1. how many trash bags each child filled; 2. Stone; 3. Tripp; 4. Wren and Renee; 5. 26.

Page 169
Answers will vary.

Page 170
1. Item is recyclable.; 2. 30; 3. 20; 4. 170.

Page 171
1. reading; 2. 6; 3. 10; 4. 6; 5. 20.

Page 172
1. 21, 28, 35, 42; 2. 21, 18, 15, 12; 3. 25, 30, 35, 40; 4. 60, 50, 40, 30; 5. 47, 57, 67, 77.

Page 173

In	Out
12	17
3	8
20	25
16	21
95	100
68	73
31	36
53	58

Page 174
Answers will vary.

Page 175
Sleeping bag order: Jimmy, Miguel, Matthew.

Page 176

Washington	Adams	Lincoln
Roosevelt	Bush	Obama

Drawings will vary.

CD-704263

Learning is just the beginning of a child's lifelong journey to success! *Second Grade Foundations* is a comprehensive guide that offers standards-based practice while reinforcing core skills for early learners. The activity pages are colorful and engaging and will provide hours of learning and fun for your child.

With *Second Grade Foundations*, your child will build a solid foundation for reading, language arts, and math through the fun and challenging cross-curricular activities in social studies and science. The extension activities on almost every page will encourage your child to utilize critical thinking and apply what he or she has learned to everyday situations.

Second Grade Foundations is your child's stepping stone to success!

AMERICAN
EDUCATION
PUBLISHING™

An imprint of Carson-Dellosa Publishing LLC
P.O. Box 35665 • Greensboro, NC 27425 USA

www.carsondellosa.com

U.S. $12.99

ISBN 13: 978-1-62399-078-7

51299

EAN

9 781623 990787

Printed in the USA